A Treatise on God's Free Grace and Man's Free Will

WILLIAM PERKINS

MONERGISM BOOKS

Copyright © 2023

A Treatise on God's Free Grace and Man's Free Will, by William Perkins

Published by by Monergism Books
P.O. Box 491
West Linn Oregon 97068
www.monergism.com

All rights reserved.

No portion of this book may be reproduced in any form without written permission from the publisher or author, except as permitted by U.S. copyright law.

ISBN: 978-1-961807-32-7

Contents

Preface	IV
To the Distinguished Sir Edward Dennie, Knight	VI
1. A Treatise on God's Free Grace and Man's Free Will	1

Preface

"A Treatise on God's Free Grace and Man's Free Will" by William Perkins offers a profound exploration of theological concepts from a Reformed perspective, particularly focusing on the interplay between divine grace and human will. Perkins, one of the foremost leaders of the Puritan movement in the Church of England during the Elizabethan era, critiques the Roman Catholic Church's views on grace and free will, arguing that they undermine the sovereignty of God's grace.

Perkins identifies two primary ways in which the Roman Catholic doctrine is seen as opposing the grace of God. Firstly, he argues that it overemphasizes the role of human free will while diminishing the role of divine grace. He contends that human will, in its natural state, is incapable of performing godly actions without being transformed by God's grace. This transformation is necessary for salvation and godliness, as human nature alone is insufficient for spiritual understanding or repentance.

Secondly, Perkins takes issue with the Catholic doctrine of synergism, which suggests that human cooperation is necessary for the efficacy of God's prevenient grace. He argues that this undermines the biblical teaching that it is God alone who enables the willing and acting according to His purpose, as stated in Philippians 2:13.

Additionally, Perkins criticizes the Catholic view that assigns a contingent will to God, dependent on human decisions. This perspective, he asserts, detracts from God's sovereignty, making human will the initiator of its own actions rather than God.

Furthermore, Perkins refutes the Catholic teaching that grace is found in the inward gifts of the mind, particularly charity. He emphasizes that true grace is not an inherent quality in humans but the free favor and mercy of God, which pardons sins and grants eternal life through Christ. This grace is not earned by works but is a gift from God.

Perkins also challenges the notion that a renewed human will, under the general direction and cooperation of God, can perform godly duties without special divine assistance. He underscores the scriptural view that it is God who works in believers both to will and to act, highlighting the continual dependence on God's grace for spiritual growth and perseverance.

He also disputes the idea that works merit grace, arguing that this contradicts the scriptural teaching that salvation is by grace alone, not works. Perkins cites biblical examples, including Abraham's faith, to illustrate that justifying grace is opposed to the works of the law.

In conclusion, Perkins advocates for a total reliance on God's grace, suggesting that all good in humans is attributed to God's grace alone. He underscores the importance of recognizing that without God's grace, humans are incapable of any spiritual good. This perspective, Perkins argues, is crucial for true godliness, peace of conscience, and salvation

To the Distinguished Sir Edward Dennie, Knight

Distinguished Sir, it is unmistakably clear that the current religious doctrine of the Church of Rome stands in opposition to the profound grace of God on two distinct fronts. First and foremost, it elevates the autonomy of man's will while diminishing the significance of divine grace. This, it accomplishes through five distinct avenues. Initially, it asserts that the natural faculty of human free will possesses not only passive or latent potential but also an active power, albeit an imperfect one, in matters of piety. In doing so, it diminishes the role of divine grace. This doctrine, in all its aspects, is fundamentally incongruent with reason. For the human will, in its inherent nature, is but a natural facet and is therefore neither suitable nor capable of effecting any supernatural deeds, as are all acts of godliness. Unless, as they suggest, it is elevated above its inherent limitations by the infusion of a supernatural disposition. Contrary to this doctrine, Scripture unequivocally proclaims, "Ye were once darkness" (Ephesians 5:8), emphasizing that we, of ourselves, are insufficient to conceive any spiritual matters (2 Corinthians 3:5). The natural person, one devoid of the Spirit of God, cannot grasp divine truths (1 Corinthians 2:14). "You were dead in sins and trespasses" (Ephesians 2:1), "without Christ and without God in the world" (verse 12). Scripture further reveals that the human heart is described as "slow" (Luke 24:25), "vain" (Psalms 5:9), "hard" and incapable of repentance (Romans 2:5), and "stony" (Ezekiel 36:26). It underscores that the Jews were obstinate, with "necks like an iron sinew" and "brows of brass" (Isaiah 48:4). It is God who grants the capacity to see with spiritual eyes and understand with an enlightened heart (Deuteronomy 29:4). Through these testimonies, it becomes manifest that divine grace not only assists our feeble nature but transforms its perverse qualities, guiding it from darkness to light (Acts 26:18) and from death to life (Ephesians 2:1). Those who fail to acknowledge this profound grace to such an extent have yet to grasp the true essence of the Gospel, nor have they contemplated the words of our Savior, Jesus Christ: "No man comes to me, unless the Father draw him" (John 6:44). Prosper, the disciple of St. Augustine, articulates a notable sentiment which, curiously, the Papists of our era seem to overlook: "We have, as he asserts, 'free will by nature, but for quality and condition, it must be transformed by our Lord Jesus Christ."

Secondly, certain adherents of the Romish faith assert that the efficacy of God's prevenient grace hinges upon the cooperation of man's will. They affirm that the Council of Trent subscribes to this perspective. However, in response to the inquiry posed by the Apostle Paul, "Who has separated thee?" (1 Corinthians 4:7), one might retort, "I have done so myself, by my own volition." Such an assertion contradicts the teaching of Paul, who asserts that beyond mere potential, the power to will rightly, ipsum velle—that is, the act of righteous volition, is granted by God (Philippians 2:13). Others propose that the efficacy of grace resides in the suitability of persuasive stimuli, as if merely inciting the heart and inclining the will towards spiritual matters would suffice to remedy our human frailty. Yet, God is known to do far more than this. He is described as softening the heart (Ezekiel 36:26), turning the heart (Luke 1:17), and opening the heart (Acts 16:14). In light of our obstinacy, He goes so far as to wound the heart (Song of Solomon 4:9) and perform circumcisions of the heart (Deuteronomy 30:6). Indeed, He even bruises the heart (Ezekiel 6:9). And when nothing else avails, God is said to remove the stony heart (Ezekiel 11:19), quicken those who are contrite (Isaiah 57:15; Ephesians 2:5), bestow a new heart (Ezekiel 36:26; Ephesians 4:23), and, most remarkably, create a new heart (Ezekiel 2:10; 4:28).

Furthermore, there exists a third aspect of their doctrine, wherein they ascribe to God, in all contingent actions, a will that depends upon the human will. They assert that God wills and determines nothing except in accordance with His foreknowledge of how the human will shall decide. In this manner, they seek to uphold the imagined freedom of the human will, characterized by its neutrality and self-determination. However, in doing so, they unwittingly strip God of His rightful honor and sovereignty. This approach places not God, but the human will itself, as the primary mover and initiator of its own actions. It is worth noting that even among some adherents of the Roman Catholic faith, this doctrine is viewed with skepticism and condemned as a mere conjecture.

Moving on to the fourth point of contention, they propagate the idea that the grace which renders us pleasing and grateful to God resides primarily in the inner qualities of the mind, particularly in the virtues of charity. Yet, this teaching is fundamentally flawed. Charity, as they assert, is indeed the fulfillment of the law. However, it is important to remember that we are no longer bound by the law but are recipients of God's grace (Romans 6:14). Furthermore, those who seek justification through the law have fallen from grace (Galatians 5:4). The grace that truly renders us pleasing to God is His unmerited favor and mercy, bestowed upon us through Christ, forgiving our sins and welcoming us into eternal life. This truth is articulated by the Apostle Paul when he declares that we are saved not by our works, but by God's purpose and grace, granted to us in Christ before the beginning of time (2 Timothy 1:9).

Lastly, they propose that the regenerated human will, with the general guidance and cooperation of God, can fulfill the obligations of godliness without the need for specific assistance from God in the form of new grace. However, the Holy Scriptures offer a contrasting perspective. "By the grace of God, I am what I am, and His grace toward me was not in vain; but I labored more abundantly than they all, yet not I, but the grace of God which was with me" (1 Corinthians 15:10). It is made clear that no one can confess Jesus as Lord except by the Holy Spirit (1 Corinthians 12:3). Jesus Himself declared, "Without me, you can do nothing" (John 15:5). The Scriptures further emphasize that after believing, we are sealed with the Holy Spirit (Ephesians 1:13) and that God, who initiated this good work in us, will bring it to completion on the day of Christ (Philippians 1:6). By the power of the Holy Spirit, we are enabled to abound in hope (Romans 15:13), and it is God who works in us both the will and the deed (Philippians 2:13). "Though the righteous fall, he shall not be cast off, for the Lord upholds him with His hand" (Psalms 37:24). We humbly beseech God to incline our hearts to His testimonies, turn our eyes from vain pursuits, and revive us in the path of righteousness (Psalms 119:36–37). We earnestly pray, "Teach me to do Your will, for You are my God; let Your good Spirit lead me on level ground" (Psalms 143:10). With heartfelt sincerity, we cry out, "Create in me a clean heart, O God, and renew a right spirit within me" (Psalms 51:10, 12). We implore God to establish us with His free spirit. We yearn for His divine guidance, saying, "Draw me, and I will run after You." Through these passages, among others, it becomes profoundly evident that after endowing us with His Spirit, God does not abandon us to our own devices. Instead, He guides, uplifts, leads, confirms, and sustains us by His unceasing grace and indwelling Spirit. Thus, as we journey in the way of His commandments, we ultimately attain the bliss of eternal happiness.

The second way in which the adherents of the papal tradition reveal their opposition to the grace of God is their inclusion of works as a co-cause in what they refer to as the second justification and the attainment of eternal life. In stark contrast, the Apostle Paul, in the context of justification, sets grace in direct opposition to works, particularly those that result from the gifts and fruits of the Spirit. Abraham did not perform righteous deeds by mere natural free will; rather, his actions were guided by faith (Hebrews 11:8). Paul underscores this by contrasting justifying grace with the works of Abraham, declaring, "To him that worketh, the wages are not counted as grace" (Romans 4:4). Additionally, Titus 3:5 reminds us that our salvation is "not by works of righteousness which we have done, but according to His mercy He saved us." Romans 11:6 reinforces this truth: "And if by grace, then it is no longer of works; otherwise grace is no longer grace." Augustine aptly asserts that grace can only be truly grace when it is freely bestowed in every way.

In light of this, it is most prudent to attribute all that is good in us or achieved by us entirely to the grace of God. Augustine eloquently proclaims, "Hold this as an unwavering principle of godliness: nothing good can originate in our senses, thoughts, or conception that is not of God." Bernard adds to this wisdom, stating, "The Church demonstrates its abundance of grace when it dedicates everything it possesses to grace, assigning it both the foremost and final place. For how can the Church truly be filled with grace if it possesses anything that is not of grace? Furthermore, I dare not claim anything as my own, lest I become my own." This doctrine provides the utmost assurance and security for our conscience and the salvation of our souls. Remarkably, even some papal theologians, while unintentionally undermining their own position, admit to this truth. Bellarmine, the Jesuit, acknowledges, "Due to the uncertainty of our own righteousness and to avoid falling into vanity, it is safest to place our complete confidence in the sole mercy and goodness of God." Cassander references Bonaventure, who wisely states, "It is the duty of devout souls to attribute nothing to themselves, but everything to the grace of God. Consequently, the more a person ascribes to the grace of God, even when surrendering many things to it, he takes nothing away from human nature and free will; he remains within the bounds of piety. However, when anything is subtracted from the grace of God and given to nature, which rightly belongs to grace, there may be cause for concern." Therefore, to firmly uphold justification by faith without reliance on works and to attribute the entire process of our conversion to God without creating divisions between grace and nature is the most secure path to follow.

I expound upon these matters in greater detail in the forthcoming treatise, which I now humbly offer to your Reverence as a conclusive expression of my devotion and affection. I kindly beseech you to accept this gift with the sincerity of my intent and to examine its contents at your convenience. In this manner, I entrust your Reverence to the care and benevolence of God in Christ.

Yours Faithfully in the Lord,
William Perkins

A Treatise on God's Free Grace and Man's Free Will

"Jerusalem, Jerusalem, which killeth the Prophets, and stoneth them which are sent to thee: how often would I have gathered thy children together, as the hen gathereth her chickens under her wings, and ye would not? Behold, your habitation shall be left to you desolate."—Matthew 23:37–38

The entirety of this chapter contains a sermon delivered by our Savior, Jesus Christ, to the Jews in Jerusalem. It can be divided into two main parts. The first part comprises a rebuke directed at the Jewish religious leaders, specifically the scribes and Pharisees. This rebuke encompasses various vices and spans from the beginning of the chapter to the thirty-sixth verse. The second part consists of a strong denunciation aimed at Jerusalem, as conveyed in the words I have just read: "Jerusalem,

Jerusalem, which killeth the prophets," and so on. In this invective, we must consider two key aspects: the rebellion of Jerusalem, as presented in verse 37, and the resulting consequences of this rebellion in verse 38.

First and foremost, let us examine the rebellion itself. Three significant aspects merit our attention: the place and the individuals involved, as indicated by the words "Jerusalem, Jerusalem"; the extent and manifestation of their rebellion, as evidenced by the phrase "which killeth the Prophets," and so forth; and the manner and form in which their rebellion unfolded, as revealed by the words "How oft would I have gathered you, and ye would not."

It is indeed a matter of wonder that Jerusalem, above all other places on Earth, should bear the weight of this grievous charge – rebellion against God. After all, Jerusalem held a unique position as the city of God, endowed with privileges that exceeded those of all other cities in the world. Saint Paul has identified seven of these privileges. First and foremost, the inhabitants were Israelites, descending from Jacob. Secondly, they were considered and referred to as the children of God – a recognition of their adoption. Thirdly, they possessed the glory of God, represented by the mercy seat, a symbol of God's presence. Fourthly, the people of Jerusalem held the covenants, including the two tables of the covenant. Fifthly, they were entrusted with the giving of the law, which included the judicial and ceremonial aspects. Sixthly, the public worship of God, marked by solemnity, was closely tied to the temple in Jerusalem. Seventhly, Jerusalem was the rightful custodian of the promises made to the patriarchs concerning the Messiah. Additionally, the prophet Micah adds an eighth privilege: the first assembly of the New Testament church would be established in Jerusalem, and consequently, the proclamation of the gospel would emanate from there to all nations (Micah 4:2).

However, despite these abundant blessings and mercies, our Savior, Jesus Christ, laments the rebellion of Jerusalem. This is not the first time He has voiced such concerns. Through the prophet Isaiah, He previously declared that, despite all His efforts on behalf of His vineyard, it yielded only wild grapes (Isaiah 5:4). In the words of the prophet Ezekiel, He cataloged His manifold blessings to His people alongside their ingratitude (Ezekiel 16). It becomes evident that where God bestows the greatest mercy, there often arises the greatest wickedness and ingratitude. We can witness a partial fulfillment of this pattern in our own time. In the span of just forty years, we have received abundant blessings from God, both for this life and the life to come, most notably the gospel accompanied by peace and protection – blessings unparalleled in earlier eras. Nevertheless, there seems to be a growing spirit of ingratitude. Many have become wearied by the gospel, distancing themselves from the fervor of their previous devotion. Regrettably, the pursuit of pleasing God and fulfilling His will is viewed by some as an overly meticulous and unnecessary endeavor.

Secondly, from this, we can deduce that God does not bind the unfailing guidance of His Spirit to any specific location or the condition of individuals. Even if any city in the world could claim such a privilege, it would have been Jerusalem. Yet, Jerusalem, the very dwelling place of God, stands accused here of rebellion against Him. Thus, no particular place or the condition of individuals possesses this privilege. Some may argue that God has made a promise to the priesthood order, stating, "The priest's lips shall preserve knowledge, and you shall require the law at his mouth" (Malachi 2:7). However, I would counter that these words do not constitute a promise but rather a command. At times, future tense words are employed in an imperative sense. Therefore, the intended meaning is, "The priest's lips shall keep," signifying, "Let them keep knowledge." Similarly, it is asserted that we are instructed to heed the scribes and Pharisees because they sit in Moses' chair (Matthew 23:2). To this, I respond that the "chair of Moses" is not a physical seat or location but rather the teachings of Moses. I grant that when this doctrine is truly taught and believed, the Spirit of God is indeed associated with it.

Thirdly, it is argued that God has promised the Spirit of truth to guide individuals into all truth (John 16:13). In response, I would clarify that this promise is not directed universally and unconditionally to all believers or all ministers. Instead, it pertains specifically to the apostles to whom it was addressed. Even then, it applies solely during their apostolic ministry, which was primarily dedicated to establishing the New Testament church through the proclamation of the gospel and the authorship of the New Testament Scriptures. In essence, no Scripture can be cited to support the notion that God has, does, or will bind His Spirit exclusively to specific places or individuals. Consequently, three erroneous beliefs held by some within the Papal tradition are undermined: First, the notion that members of the Catholic church cannot err, even though they may significantly err, when gathered in a properly convened general council. Second, the idea that the Pope is infallible in his consistory. Third, the concept that personal succession serves as a definitive mark of the Catholic church, even though it can be separated from the Spirit of God, as history demonstrates.

When our Savior, Jesus Christ, employs repetition, as in "O Jerusalem, Jerusalem," He conveys three distinct messages. Firstly, He conveys His astonishment and incredulity at the Jews' profound ingratitude despite the abundant blessings they have received. Secondly, through this repetition, He expresses His strong disapproval of their ingratitude. Thirdly, by repeating this address, He calls the Jews to wake from their spiritual slumber, provoking them to deep introspection and a profound sense of disgust toward their sin. This proclamation also serves as a reminder to us. This emphasis is not without reason, as ingratitude encompasses two grave sins against God: false testimony and injustice. Ingratitude involves false testimony because the ungrateful individual, in his heart, denies that God is the source and giver of the blessings he has received. Instead, he attributes these blessings to his own wisdom, goodness, strength, and efforts. Additionally, ingratitude is an act of injustice because it withholds from God the due reverence and gratitude owed to Him for His benevolent gifts.

The second aspect that warrants our reflection is the extent of the rebellion seen among the Jews. David, in his wisdom, delineates three levels of rebellion. Firstly, it involves walking in the counsel of the ungodly. Secondly, it includes standing in the path of sinners. Thirdly, it culminates in taking a seat among the scoffers (Psalm 1:1). This represents the pinnacle of desperate rebellion, and it mirrors the sin of Jerusalem. When Christ declares, "Which killest the Prophets, and stonest them which are sent to thee," He exposes three grievous sins within this city: impenitence, signifying their persistence in wickedness without any intention of repentance; sacrilegious and profane contempt of God and the means of salvation; and cruelty, manifested through the shedding of innocent blood. When I speak of cruelty, I do not refer to one or two isolated acts but rather to a habitual pattern—a custom of bloodshed.

Now, one may wonder how the Jews descended to such depths of wickedness. Allow me to provide an answer. In every actual sin, there are four distinct components to consider: the fault, which constitutes an offense against God in any action; the guilt or the liability to punishment for the fault; the punishment itself, which often takes the form of death; and a blemish or stain imprinted on the soul of the sinner as a consequence of the fault or offense. This blemish is nothing other than a propensity toward the committed sin or even other sins. In the case of our first parents' transgression, in addition to the fault, guilt, and punishment, there emerged a blemish or deformity within their souls. This deformity entailed the loss of God's image and an inclination of their hearts toward various forms of evil.

Since the fall of Adam, anyone who commits an actual offense, in addition to the fault, guilt, and punishment, inscribes in their heart a new blemish. This blemish takes the form of an intensified natural inclination toward sin. It is analogous to the drunkard who, with each indulgence, augments his capacity for drinking, further fueling his thirst. Therefore, the Jews, through their habitual transgressions, ultimately reached the zenith of wickedness. Every act of sin left its mark, and the accumulation of sinful acts led to a continuous augmentation of the blemish or flaw within the soul. This progression persists until the light of one's inherent moral compass is extinguished, ultimately leading to a reprobate mindset. This serves as a solemn admonition to all individuals to exercise caution and avoid committing any offense against God, whether in thought, word, or deed. Every offense leaves an indelible mark on the soul.

Secondly, one may inquire how Jerusalem, having reached such a pinnacle of rebellion, could still be referred to as "the holy City" [Matthew 27:53] or "the City of the great King" [Matthew 5:35]. I offer two explanations. First, within Jewry and Jerusalem, there resided numerous righteous men and women who genuinely feared God and eagerly anticipated the arrival of Christ's kingdom. Among them were individuals like Joseph, Mary, Zachariah, Elisabeth, Anna, Simeon, Nicodemus, Joseph of Arimathea, and many others. In designating a church or community, it is not the larger but the more virtuous segment that holds significance—just as a heap of grain retains its name, even when there is more chaff than wheat. Secondly, I propose that a people or congregation that has strayed from God continues to be regarded as such until God Himself abandons them, much like an adulterous wife remains a presumed wife until her husband issues a formal divorce decree. Indeed, Jerusalem had turned away from God, but God had not yet forsaken Jerusalem. There, He still preserved the temple and His worship. Even after Jerusalem had condemned and crucified Christ, the Apostle Peter, guided by the Holy Spirit, affirmed, "The promise is for you and for your children" [Acts 2:39]. Jerusalem did not cease to be a city or congregation of God until they contradicted and blasphemed the apostolic ministry, prompting the apostles to distance themselves from the Jews. In this, we witness the profound extent of God's mercy. Although the Jews had repeatedly deserved abandonment due to their actions, God did not forsake them. He continued to extend His mercy toward them. This serves as a lesson for us not to prematurely judge evil individuals, for while they may have turned away from God, we do not know if God has abandoned them.

From the example of Jerusalem's rebellion, we can draw several lessons. Firstly, it reveals the inherent depravity of human nature and our innate proclivity towards sin. The Jews sought to suppress and extinguish the message of salvation—going so far as to quench it with blood, even the blood of the prophets. This demonstrates that humanity readily embraces iniquity, much like a fish submerged in water.

Secondly, in the rebellion of Jerusalem, we may discern the dire state of the Church of Rome in our present day. It exceeds even the rebellion of Jerusalem. Upon impartial examination, one may conclude that "the whore of Babylon" refers to the current Church of Rome. This "whore" is described as being intoxicated with the blood of the saints. The locusts emerging from the bottomless pit are sent to stir the kings of the earth into waging war against the Church of God. These locusts are likely symbolic of monks, friars, and Jesuits belonging to the Church of Rome. Through extensive and prolonged experience, we have observed that the Roman Catholic Church has harbored a deep thirst for the blood of both rulers and the populace in this land.

Thirdly, we find here a profound lesson in the practice of meekness, goodness, and peace toward all people. The prophet Isaiah foretells that in the kingdom of Christ, individuals will no longer wield their swords and spears to harm others, as the Jews did in this instance. Instead, they will repurpose these weapons into tools for tilling the soil, such as mattocks and plowshares (Isaiah 2:4). This symbolism signifies that those who are genuinely reborn will renounce any intention or inclination to cause harm and will devote themselves to doing good. Isaiah also prophesies that "the wolf and the lamb shall dwell together, and there shall be no harm in all the holy mount of God" (Isaiah 65:25). The devil, through the sin of our first parents, turned us into beasts—lions, wolves, tigers, bears, and serpents. However, Christ, through His grace, transforms us into His lambs and sheep in terms of meekness and patience.

Fourthly, we are instructed not to resist the ministers of God but, with humility and without arrogance, to submit and obey their ministry. Isaiah prophesies that in the New Testament church, a little child—referring to ministers who may be perceived as weak or unassuming—shall, through their teaching, guide and govern wolves, leopards, and lions, symbolizing individuals with fiery and cruel natures by default. "My people," declares the Lord, "shall come willingly on the day of assembly," and the sheep of Christ recognize His voice and follow Him. While the Jews arraign and judge the prophets sent to them, we must allow them to carry out their ministry of correction and judgment upon us, lest we face judgment from the Lord. Furthermore, the Jews may have condemned their teachers, but we must allow our teachers, in a sense, to correct us. Their ministry should serve as a refining tool, like a sacrificial knife, to put to death the old, sinful nature within us, making us a pleasing offering to God.

Lastly, ministers of the word must draw strength from this passage and not be disheartened if they encounter hatred and persecution from people. After all, even the holy prophets of God faced such challenges, and this occurred within the city of Jerusalem itself.

The third aspect to consider is the manner or form of their rebellion. In this, I will examine four elements: the will of God against which the Jews rebelled: "I would"; the will of the Jews in rebellion: "you would not"; the harmony of both: "I would, but you would not"; and the nature of God's will—He desires their salvation with love, "I would have gathered you as a hen gathers her chicks," and with patience, "How often would I?" Before delving into these points individually, let me provide a general introduction concerning the nature of will.

Will is the power of desiring, refusing, choosing, and abstaining, dependent on reason. When I say "power," I mean the capacity or inherent faculty. In humans and angels, this power is proper, but in God, it is analogous or proportional, as His will is His essence or divinity itself. Secondly, I mention that it is a "power of desiring, refusing, choosing, and abstaining" because these are the direct effects of will, distinguishing it from other faculties. Lastly, I note that it "depends on reason" because it is exclusive to rational beings—God, angels, and humans. Even when will acts contrary to sound reason, it does so with a form of reasoning. In every act of will, two elements are present: reason to guide and choice to consent or dissent.

Will possesses its distinctive quality—liberty of the will—which is freedom from coercion or force but not from all necessity. It is free from coercion because coercion and will are fundamentally opposed, and where coercion exists, will ceases. Constrained will is not true will. Nonetheless, will and necessity can coexist. God wills many things out of absolute necessity, such as the eternal generation of the Son, the procession of the Holy Spirit, and the administration of justice, while preserving perfect freedom of will. The good angels will their own happiness and the practice of justice out of necessity, as they cannot will to sin or suffer misery, and they do so with the utmost freedom. In fact, the necessity of not sinning is the glory and adornment of will, for one who does good in such a way that they cannot sin is freer in doing good than someone who can choose either good or evil. When the creature willingly serves God and cannot do otherwise, it attains perfect liberty. However, since the fall of humanity, the liberty of will is coupled with a necessity to sin because it remains in bondage to sin. For this reason, Augustine aptly termed it "the bond free will." Therefore, we should not conceive of will as possessing a liberty free from all necessity. To better understand this, let us examine various types of necessity.

First, there is simple or absolute necessity, where something cannot be otherwise. For example, we can say that there is a God, and He is righteous. This necessity does not negate the creature's will but remains consistent with God's will, where an absolute necessity for holiness and goodness is combined with absolute freedom of will. Second, there is necessity by force or compulsion, which eradicates freedom and the consent of the will. Third, there is necessity by infallibility or consequence, where something necessarily follows from a given antecedent, such as God's determination and decree. Both this necessity and freedom of will can coexist. In voluntary actions, it suffices that they originate from judgment and have their inception within the will, even though they possess unchangeable necessity in relation to God's will. The certainty of God's decree does not negate the consent of human will but rather directs and gently inclines it. Coercion is the only thing directly opposed to freedom of will as it eradicates consent.

The freedom of will manifests itself in two forms. The first is when it can desire something to be as it is and simultaneously be able to desire the opposite—an aspect known in academic circles as "the liberty of contradiction." The second is when it can will something to have the ability to desire another thing or its opposite. For instance, when God willed the creation of the world, He could have also willed its non-creation, or when He willed the creation of one world, He could have willed the creation of more worlds. This is referred to as the "liberty of contrariety."

This distinction sets human will apart from the inclinations of natural agents, which consistently act in the same manner. For instance, put matter in the presence of fire, and it will invariably burn—it cannot do otherwise. Likewise, when you throw a stone into the air, it will always fall back down, incapable of any other action. Second, human will distinguishes itself from the appetites of animals, which are directed by their senses and maintain a consistent pattern when choosing or refusing. Sheep instinctively flee from wolves, and this holds true for all sheep, everywhere, at all times. Bees unfailingly collect honey—this behavior is constant and unalterable. Even when an animal in the field appears to choose one herb and reject another, it only appears to have a form of liberty. In reality, it consistently chooses or refuses in the same manner each time.

Now, let's turn to the specific topic at hand. The first aspect concerns the will of Christ: "I would." In Christ, there exist two wills corresponding to His two natures—the will of His divinity and the will of His humanity. Some argue that these words pertain to the will of His humanity, as they consider Him to speak as the minister of circumcision and thus as a human being (Rom. 15:8). While this perspective holds some truth, it does not encompass the whole truth. This is because what He willed—namely, the gathering of Jews through the ministry of the prophets—had already been initiated and practiced long before His incarnation. Therefore, in this context, it is His divine will that is primarily referred to, which is also the will of the Father and the Holy Spirit.

This divine will is singular, just as God is one, yet it can be distinguished in the following manner: it is either the will of His good pleasure or His declarative will. This distinction finds its parallel in earthly rulers, who bear the likeness of God. A king determines within himself, based on his own pleasure, what will be done in his realm and what will not—this is his will. Furthermore, he communicates some aspects of his concealed intentions to his subjects as circumstances warrant, and this too is considered his will. Similarly, the divine pleasure of God, either held within Himself or communicated to His creation, in whole or in part, constitutes His will.

The first point is found in Ephesians 1:5, where Paul mentions that the Ephesians were predestined according to the good pleasure of His will. To understand this fully, let's delve into four key aspects of this divine will. Firstly, this will represents God's purpose or decree, formulated through His divine counsel. His counsel encompasses all things and their underlying causes, while His decree determines what shall occur and what shall not, all in accordance with His eternal counsel. However, God's counsel is not a governing rule over His will, for there exists nothing higher than His will itself. Moreover, His counsel aligns with His will, which is inherently good. Paul even refers to it as "the counsel of his will" (Eph. 1:11).

Secondly, God's will contains an aspect of sovereignty—a supreme and absolute power that enables Him to govern all actions as He pleases. He wills of His own accord, independent of any external influence or constraint, and His will is unimpeded, uncontrolled, determining what, when, and how things will occur. This sovereignty is illustrated in the parable, "May I not do with mine own as I will?" (Matthew 20:15), and is further emphasized by Paul when he quotes Moses, saying, "I will have mercy on whom I will have mercy" (Romans 9:15). This underscores that we are entirely subject to God's pleasure, much like clay in the hands of a potter. Consequently, when we discuss God's works and judgments, we should do so with humility, sobriety, admiration, and reverence. We must refrain from probing the reasons behind them or judging them harshly when they don't align with our human reasoning. Instead, we should rest assured that God possesses the ultimate sovereignty over His will, and His will is inherently good.

The third point to understand is that God's will serves as the primal cause of all things, leaving nothing exempt—neither their existence nor their actions and motions. This first-cause status manifests in two ways: firstly, in regard to the existence of things; secondly, in regard to their goodness. To illustrate that everything derives its existence from the will of God as the primary efficient cause, consider this: God's power is such that nothing can occur contrary to His will, or entirely against it. Hence, whatever comes to pass, does so because He either wills it wholly or in part. In a similar vein, a wise ruler of a household or army, having absolute power, allows nothing to transpire without his will, even in the simplest matters. He desires to have a say in everything. Nothing hampers this desire except his own limitations—a weakness that doesn't apply to God's majesty. God possesses unchangeable foreknowledge of all that will transpire, and consequently, He unchangeably wills their occurrence. God's foreknowledge depends on His will, not the other way around—He foresees events because they are determined to occur according to His will. While God has knowledge of events that could possibly happen but never do, this knowledge precedes His decree. However, His knowledge of events that will unquestionably happen follows His will and determination. It is essential to understand that God's willing results in the actualization of things—His will and His power are intrinsically connected. When He wills something, He brings it into being. Hence, the Holy Spirit signifies the will of God through an operational word or command, as in "In the beginning God said, let there be this and that, and it was so" (Genesis 1). This divine command is equivalent to His will becoming reality. Furthermore, human beings subsist by every word of God, meaning they rely on whatever God, in His pleasure, wills to be their sustenance. In essence, things concerning their existence either depend on God's will or on themselves or other entities. If they rely on themselves, they become gods. If they depend on any entity other than God, that entity becomes god. Therefore, the conclusion is that everything, in terms of existence and actions, depends on God as the highest cause or the cause of all causes. This foundational doctrine should be remembered, for it forms the basis of genuine patience. When we understand that everything that occurs happens according to God's will, we can find solace. Job armed himself with patience, saying, "The Lord gave, and the Lord hath taken away; blessed be the name of the Lord" (Job 1:21). Likewise, David found comfort when he acknowledged that God was the source of his afflictions, stating, "I held my tongue, I spake not; because thou Lord didst it" (Psalm 39:9). Secondly, this doctrine offers profound consolation when we realize that all our afflictions originate from God's good pleasure. The early Christian church found solace in this understanding, knowing that the actions of Jews, Herod, Pontius Pilate, and others did not contravene God's counsel. Instead, these actions aligned with God's predetermined plan (Acts 4:28). It is a comfort to us that we are predestined to become conformed to the image of Christ in our afflictions (Romans 8:29; Philippians 3:10).

Moreover, it is essential to recognize that the goodness of all things begins with the will of God. A thing is not inherently good and then subsequently willed by God; rather, it is first willed by God, and in His will, it becomes good. This truth is evident and need not be debated. However, an important question arises: where does evil, particularly sin, find its origin? I answer that sin emanates from the will of the fallen creature and not from the will of God, yet it is not without the knowledge of God. While God does not will sin in the proper sense because He abhors it, He does will its existence in the world. In the divine counsel of God, it is deemed good for evil to exist. God wills the presence of sin not because He actively seeks to produce or give it existence, but because His will is to withdraw from His creature and not obstruct the emergence of evil when He has the power to do so. Consequently, unimpeded evil comes into being. Although God foresaw sin in His eternal counsel and chose not to hinder it when He could have, He effectively willed its existence in the world, albeit not in a straightforward manner.

The final point to consider is that God's good pleasure, concealed from us, does not serve as the rule for our actions and faith. As Moses stated, "Secret things belong to the Lord our God, but the things revealed belong to us and to our children" (Deuteronomy 29:29). Consequently, we may, with humility and submission, dissent from this hidden will of God before it becomes known to us without committing sin. Paul, acting in accordance with his apostolic commission, intended to preach in Asia and Bithynia, but the Spirit prevented him. In this instance, Paul did not sin. It is worth noting that one good intention may differ from another, and what a creature sometimes desires without offense may be willed differently by God according to His righteous pleasure. Samuel prayed for Saul in a manner inconsistent with God's secret will, but he ceased his supplication once the decree of God was revealed to him. Here, we must admonish those who reason that if it is God's will for them to be saved, they will be saved regardless of how they live. Such individuals make the secret will of God the guiding principle of their lives, which should not be the case. The revealed will of God constitutes the law and sole standard for both actions and beliefs.

Consequently, it is evident that the will of God's pleasure mentioned in this text, "How often would I?" does not refer to a will that cannot be resisted or opposed. "My counsel shall stand, and I will do all my pleasure" (Isaiah 46:10) affirms that the pleasure of God is irresistible. However, the will mentioned here can indeed be resisted and opposed: "I would, but you would not."

Furthermore, the signifying will of God is when He reveals some portion of His pleasure, to the extent that it benefits His creatures and manifests His justice or mercy. While this signifying will is not God's will in the strictest sense, as His will of good pleasure is, it can still rightly be referred to as His will. Just as the effects of anger in God are termed "anger" even in the absence of the actual emotion, so too can the sign and indication of His will be labeled as "will."

God's signifying will is often conveyed in various degrees of clarity. It is presented more explicitly in three ways: through His word, His permission, and His actions.

Firstly, God's word is an expression of His will, as affirmed by Paul when he encouraged, "Prove what is the good will of God" (Romans 12:2). This represents not His decree or pleasure, but His revealing will, as it serves to communicate what is pleasing and acceptable to God, what is expected of us, and what He demands of us if we seek eternal life. The commandments, prohibitions, promises, and threats found in both the law and the gospel, as well as the entire dispensation of His word, are expressions of God's signifying will. Commandments convey what we are to do, prohibitions guide us away from what we should avoid, promises reveal the good God intends for us, and threats forewarn us of the consequences of sin. Additionally, the ministry and dispensation of God's word serve as expressions of His signifying will, communicating His intentions regarding the salvation of humanity. Divine permission is likewise a manifestation of God's signifying will, indicating that He will not obstruct the occurrence of that which is permitted.

Thirdly, every work or action of God communicates His intentions and what must come to pass. When an action is completed, we discern the pleasure of God, for nothing transpires without His will. When the signifying will is less clearly presented, it may seem that there is a contradiction between the signifying will and God's will of good pleasure. However, in reality, there is no contradiction. God conceals some aspects of His will to promote the well-being of His creatures. Scripture provides examples of this concealment, falling into three categories.

Firstly, God may present a command to humans while concealing the purpose behind it. Divine precepts generally serve one of three purposes: obedience, testing, or conviction. Obedience involves fulfilling the command exactly as given, testing examines the loyalty of the creature without demanding the specific action, and conviction aims to demonstrate disobedience. For instance, parents sometimes issue commands to their children that must be obeyed, while at other times, they issue commands to assess their children's affection and duty. Occasionally, one person may command another as a means of conviction, revealing disobedience. Divine precepts fall into three categories: precepts of obedience, precepts of testing, and precepts of conviction. When the purpose behind a precept is concealed, God's pleasure is conveyed less clearly. For example, God commanded Abraham to "Offer your only son Isaac" (Genesis 22:2). The purpose of this command was to test Abraham, a purpose that was concealed until he was in the process of obeying the command. When the Angel of the Lord intervened and said, "Now I see that you fear God" (Genesis 22:12), it became evident that the command was intended for testing, not for the actual sacrifice of Isaac. Though the command appeared to contradict God's will of good pleasure or decree, there was no real contradiction, as it was decreed that Isaac would not be sacrificed and that Abraham would be tested in offering him. Consequently, this command aligns with God's decree, as it serves as a command of testing. Similarly, God instructed Pharaoh, "Let my people go" (Exodus 8:1), yet His secret purpose was that Pharaoh would not release them. Although this may seem contradictory on the surface, it is not. God also decreed that Pharaoh would be convinced of his rebellion and hard-heartedness, and this command served that purpose. While, from Pharaoh's perspective, it was a command to be obeyed and fulfilled, for God, it was primarily a command of conviction.

Through this doctrine, the public ministry of the word is firmly defended. Some hold the belief that it serves to deceive the world because it issues a universal command for all to repent and believe, while the grace to do so is not universally given. However, this perspective is misguided. While the command "repent and believe," in the minister's intention, aims at the salvation of all, in God's intention and counsel, it serves various purposes. For those ordained to eternal life, it constitutes a precept of obedience because God empowers them to fulfill what He commands. For others, it serves as a command of trial or conviction, revealing their sin and leaving no room for excuses. Thus, when the command to believe is given without the accompanying grace of faith, it is not a means of delusion but rather a means of reproving and convicting individuals of their unbelief, done so in God's justice.

The second instance of God's signifying will being darkly conveyed occurs when God presents promises, concealing the exceptions or conditions attached to them. For instance, when God declared, "You shall have dominion over the birds of the air, the fish of the sea," etc. (Genesis 1:28), and when He proclaimed concerning Jerusalem, "This is my resting place forever" (Psalm 132:14), these promises do not currently come to fruition. However, there is no contradiction in God's will because these promises must be understood with their exceptions, such as "unless you fall away from me and provoke my anger through your sins."

The third example arises when God presents His threats while concealing the conditions and exceptions. He declared, "I will not save you anymore" (Judges 10:13), and yet He later chose to deliver them repeatedly. Similarly, God said, "Leave me alone, that my anger may burn against them, and I may consume them" (Exodus 32:10), but He spared them at the intercession of Moses. Furthermore, He pronounced, "Yet forty days, and Nineveh shall be overthrown" (Jonah 3:4), but Nineveh was spared and not destroyed. In these cases, there should be no notion of change or falsehood in God's character. All threats proclaimed must be understood with the clause "unless you repent and turn to me" (Ezekiel 18). God conceals this exception to better instill fear in the consciences of individuals and prepare them for genuine repentance (Isaiah 38). For example, when the prophet told Hezekiah, "Set your house in order, for you shall die; you shall not recover" (2 Kings 20:1; Isaiah 38:1), Hezekiah lived fifteen more years. In this situation, God concealed His own purpose, indicating what would happen to Hezekiah based on natural considerations and human remedies. In all these examples, there should be no suspicion of deception or deceit on God's part. He does not speak one thing while secretly intending another, as hypocrites might. Instead, He conceals part of His will while revealing another part, all for the benefit of humanity.

Now, let us turn our attention to the text at hand. The words "I would have gathered you" should not be understood as expressing God's decree but rather as His signifying will, specifically through the ministry of the word. When God sent His word to Jerusalem through His prophets, He signified His desire and will to gather and convert them. God is said to will the conversion of the Jews through His word in two ways. First, He approved it as intrinsically good, aligning with His own goodness and mercy. Second, He commanded and demanded it of them as their duty and a necessary step for salvation. Some might argue that it seems unjust for God to command the Jews to do something they are unable to do and then complain when they are not gathered, comparing it to a master commanding a servant to carry a mountain on his back and lamenting when it remains undone. However, this analogy does not apply here. If a master could grant his servant the power and ability to carry a mountain, he could indeed command it. If, due to the servant's own fault, he lost this ability, the master could still command him and justly complain if the command was not obeyed. This parallels God's situation: He originally bestowed grace upon all people through our first ancestors, enabling them to obey His commandments. However, humanity has rejected this grace and no longer desires it from God. Therefore, God is under no obligation to restore this grace. He can rightfully command us to turn to Him, even though we are currently unable to do so.

When we compare this text with Isaiah 6:10, they may appear contradictory. In this passage, Christ states, "I would have gathered you," while in Isaiah, He declares, "Harden them so that they cannot be gathered and converted." It may seem as though God both wills and does not will the same thing. However, there is only one divine will in God, yet it does not will all things equally. Instead, it wills and does not will the same thing in different respects. God wills the conversion of Jerusalem in that He approves it as intrinsically good, commands it, encourages people to do it, and provides them with external means for conversion. However, He does not will it in the sense of decreeing to work their conversion effectively. God can approve and require many things without necessarily carrying them out, based on reasons known only to Himself. For instance, God approved the confirmation of the angels that fell as a good thing in itself but did not will to confirm them. Similarly, a compassionate judge may approve and will the life of a criminal but also will the execution of justice through the criminal's death. Thus, God may sometimes will in His signifying will what He does not will in His will of good pleasure.

From this explanation, we learn that when God establishes the ministry of His word, it signifies His desire to gather people to salvation. This aligns with the words of the prophet Isaiah, who likened the preaching of the gospel to "a banner displayed" (Isaiah 49:22), inviting all nations to come to it. In our English nation, this truth has been evident for more than forty years, as God has unfurled this banner and signified His will for mercy and salvation through the ministry of His word. Therefore, we owe God gratitude and praise for His boundless mercy. We should also show reverence for the ministry of the word, recognizing it as a means through which God reveals His good will to us. In all obedience, we should submit ourselves to it and allow ourselves to be converted and gathered by it. Just as subjects respect their king's decrees, we must hold in even higher regard the word of the living God sent to us through the ministry and align ourselves with it. Lastly, we should recognize the dire state of our land. Despite God's clear signaling of His will for our eternal good, many among us neglect or despise the gospel. In most places, people have grown weary of it, similar to the Israelites' weariness with manna. Yet, our weariness of God's goodness, which offers and proclaims mercy, only leads us closer to our own destruction.

It is also crucial to note that Jerusalem's rebellion is directed against Christ's signifying will when He says, "I would, but you would not." This implies that the signifying will of God should guide our obedience, not the concealed will. Therefore, whenever God signifies His will to us, whether through His commandments and prohibitions, through His permission, or through His operations, we must obey. We are instructed to say, "Thy will be done," not only in response to the will revealed in His Word but also in response to His will revealed through events. When something occurs, it happens because it was God's will. Thus, in all circumstances, we should find our solace and patience in His signifying will.

Thirdly, let us consider the implications for ministers and teachers of the Word. They must cast aside any self-serving motives related to profit or praise and, with sincere hearts, dedicate themselves and their ministry to the paramount objective of gathering people to God. For what is the master's intent in any undertaking must also be the servant's intent. The master's intent is clearly articulated here: "How often I would have gathered you."

Now, let's delve into the second point, which is understanding the will of man. To grasp this, we must explore two facets: the nature of man's will and the extent of its strength. We've already touched upon the nature of the will in a general sense, but there is more to add. We can discern the nature of man's will through its practical expression. The practical manifestation of the will involves five key elements. First, there is the mental process of considering the action to be taken and its ultimate purpose. Second, comes the deliberation over various means to achieve the desired end. Third, following deliberation, a decision is made regarding what course of action should be pursued. Fourth, we have the specific function of the will itself, which is the act of choosing or refusing based on the determination made by the mind—essentially, it's where the will decides what shall be done and what shall not. Finally, the fifth aspect highlights the will's inherent liberty. When the will chooses or rejects something, it does so freely, without external coercion. Even after making a choice, it retains the natural capacity to reverse that choice and opt for an alternative course.

Furthermore, it's crucial to distinguish between man's will and his capacity to carry out his intentions. In God, will and power are indistinguishable since they constitute His essence. What God can will, He can accomplish; what He wills, He brings to fruition. His act of willing is synonymous with His act of doing. However, the situation differs in the case of humans. A person can will something that they lack the ability to execute. As the apostle Paul stated, "To will is present with me, but how to perform what is good I do not find within myself" (Romans 7:18). Thus, will is one facet, and the power to execute the willed action is another.

The second aspect we must explore is the capability of the will – what it can and cannot do, and the extent of its reach. To understand this, we shall examine the will in four distinct states of humanity: the state of innocence before the fall, the state of corruption after the fall, the state of regeneration following conversion, and the state of glory beyond this earthly life.

In the state of innocence, the human will possessed the power to choose between good and evil. God issued a command to Adam, prohibiting him from eating the fruit of the tree of knowledge of good and evil. Adam had the capacity to either obey or disobey this command. This no longer applies to us after the fall, but it was applicable to Adam because God endowed him with the ability to obey. Adam's failure to obey demonstrated the outcome. As Ecclesiastes tells us, "God made man upright" (Eccl. 7:29). Adam possessed the power to choose what was good, but he also had the power to choose evil. Moses, speaking to the Israelites, said, "I have set before you life and death, blessing and cursing; therefore choose life, that both you and your descendants may live" (Deuteronomy 30:19). These words prescribe what should be done, not what we are capable of doing now. Adam had the ability to choose both good and evil, a gift from God at his creation before the fall.

In Adam's will, two elements were present: liberty and mutability. Liberty had two dimensions. The first was the freedom to will, not to will, or to suspend judgment, grounded in the nature of the will itself. This is a natural liberty, inseparable from the essence of the will. It remains even in the damned spirits because without this liberty, there can be no will.

The second form of liberty is the liberty of grace, which is the ability to choose what is good and reject what is evil, to will what is right and to reject wrongdoing. This liberty does not derive from the nature of the will but from its inherent goodness, or holiness, which is a reflection of God's image. We must be cautious not to entertain the notion that Adam was created in a state of neither righteousness nor unrighteousness, but in a middle ground between the two. This contradicts the apostle's teaching that man was created in righteousness and holiness (Ephesians 4:24; Colossians 3:10). In this initial state of Adam's creation, he possessed the liberty of grace. This second form of liberty also granted Adam freedom from sin and freedom from misery.

The mutability of Adam's will is evident in the fact that although it was created as good, it had the potential to change, influenced by the force of temptation. To understand the cause of this mutability, consider that for a creature created in righteousness to remain eternally and consistently righteous, two divine aids are required. Firstly, there must be the power to persevere in goodness; without this power, a creature's inherent goodness would cease. Secondly, there must be an act or choice, the will to persevere or the act of perseverance itself. Both of these aids are necessary. God bestows the power and the will to do good, as well as the action of doing good. A creature does not perform the good it can do unless God enables it, just as God grants the capacity to do good.

The righteous angels possess both of these divine aids and, as a result, they stand firm. However, Adam received only the first aid from God, the power to persist in righteousness, if he so chose. The act of perseverance was left to his own free will.

One might argue that if Adam received the power to do good but not the will to exercise that power, then he did not receive sufficient grace. To this, we respond that Adam did receive sufficient grace for the perfection of his nature, for full obedience to God's will, and for attaining eternal happiness, provided he did not fail to cooperate. However, he did not receive the grace necessary for absolute immutability of his nature, nor was it necessary to bestow such grace upon a creature.

Consider this analogy: A skilled jeweler intends to craft a priceless jewel using gold, pearls, and precious stones. After achieving perfection, the jeweler does not impose a condition upon the jewel that it will remain unscathed if it falls. Likewise, God created Adam in a state of perfection, granting him the ability and capacity to maintain that perfection, should he choose to do so. However, God did not impose upon Adam the condition of absolute immutability and unchangeability when faced with external temptations.

The practical application of the former doctrine is profound. In Adam's example, we witness the frailty of even the most excellent creature when devoid of God's grace. Despite having the power to persevere, Adam could not, on his own, put that power into action. He could fall by his own volition but could not stand or rise again without divine assistance. In light of this, we, as sinful beings, should humbly acknowledge our weakness and attribute all the good we do or can do to the grace of God. This has been the practice of the godly throughout history. The repentant Jews cried out, "Convert thou me, and I will be converted" (Jeremiah 31:18). The bride of Christ implores, "Draw us, and we will run after thee" (Song of Solomon 1:4). King David pleads, "Incline my heart to thy commandments; turn mine eyes from the beholding of vanity, and quicken me in thy precepts" (Psalm 119:36–37). Augustine wisely declares, "Give that which Thou commandest, and command what Thou wilt." Considering our frailty, it is best for us to deny ourselves and, through faith, depend on the providence and mercy of God.

Furthermore, those who believe in Christ have every reason to be thankful to God, as they receive the beginnings of a greater grace than Adam ever knew. While Adam received only the power to persevere in his happy state if he chose to do so, believers receive not only the power but also the will and the deed to run the race toward eternal life, as Paul attests: "Work out your own salvation with fear and trembling; for it is God who works in you both to will and to do for His good pleasure" (Philippians 2:13).

In the state of corruption, we must consider two aspects of man's will: what it is capable of achieving and how close it can come to accomplishing a good work, as well as what it cannot do. To elucidate the former, we must explore two facets of a corrupted will: liberty and possibility. Liberty denotes a certain freedom to will or refuse or suspend one's will. This liberty remains since the fall of Adam and is intrinsic to the will, inseparable from its nature. This liberty manifests itself in three categories of actions: natural, human, and ecclesiastical.

Natural actions are shared by both humans and animals, such as eating, drinking, sleeping, smelling, hearing, tasting, and moving. It is evident through common experience that freedom to will exists in all these actions.

Human actions encompass activities common to all individuals and can be categorized into three groups. Firstly, there are pursuits related to arts, trades, occupations, and various professions. Experience affirms that individuals possess the freedom to will in all these areas. Secondly, there is the governance of societies, including families and commonwealths. The Lord informed Cain regarding Abel, "Thou shalt rule over him" (Genesis 4:7), signifying that Cain had the liberty of will to exercise dominion over his brother, with Abel's will being subject to his own. Peter noted that Ananias had the choice to give or withhold his lands of his own will before making the offering (Acts 5:4). Additionally, Paul acknowledged that fathers have "power over their own will" (1 Corinthians 7:37) concerning the marriage of their children. Lastly, there is the practice of civil virtues such as justice, temperance, liberality, and chastity. Paul remarked that Gentiles "by nature do the things contained in the law" (Romans 2:14). To be outwardly chaste, just, bountiful, and so forth is within the capacity of a natural and corrupted will. Some may argue that these virtues are gifts of the Holy Ghost. In response, it must be clarified that the gifts of the Holy Ghost can be divided into two categories: gifts of restraint and gifts of renovation. Gifts of restraint serve only to curb the corruption of nature, not to mortify or eliminate it. They are common to all individuals, both good and bad, and exist to maintain outward peace and order in human societies. Civil virtues fall into this category. Conversely, gifts of renovation are graces of the Holy Ghost that not only restrain the corruption of the inner person but also mortify it at its root, effecting a transformation of our sinful nature. These virtues are exclusively granted to those who are in Christ.

The third category of actions pertains to ecclesiastical duties, specifically those involving the outward worship of God. Even in these matters, there exists a liberty of will. Corrupt and sinful individuals possess the power and freedom to contemplate God, entertain thoughts that are inherently good [Romans 1:21], read and explore the Scriptures [2 Corinthians 3:14], engage in discussions regarding the word of God [Psalm 50:16], attend congregational gatherings, and display a semblance of zeal (not necessarily righteous but, indeed, a form of zeal) for the external aspects of religious observance. Paul noted that the unyielding Jews had "a zeal for God" and adhered to the law's righteousness [James 2:19]. Additionally, he, as an unconverted Pharisee, deemed himself "blameless concerning the righteousness which is in the law" [Philippians 3:6]. Such is the extent of human capability through the liberty of a corrupted will. It is worth noting that the devil, by natural strength, can even go further. He is said to possess belief, albeit not bestowed through the illumination of the Spirit of God, as in the case of humanity, but rather by clinging to the remnants of natural light and the enduring power within his corrupted will. It is essential to understand that, following his fall, he is not enlightened in any way by the Spirit of God.

This understanding reveals the limitations of a corrupted will. We must further recognize that it is replete with weaknesses and deficiencies, which can be summarized in three principles:

1. What the will desires, it cannot accomplish unless it aligns with God's will. Hence, the exhortation in the epistle of James to say, "We will do this or that, if the Lord wills" [James 4:15]. Similarly, Paul, while expressing his desire for a successful journey to Rome, added the clause "if it is God's will" [Romans 15:32]. Notably, Herod, Pontius Pilate, and the Jewish authorities did nothing against Christ that had not been determined by the counsel of God beforehand [Acts 4:28].

2. What the will desires, it cannot achieve without the assistance of God, for "in Him we live and move and have our being" [Acts 17:28]. This divine help takes two forms: the preservation of the will, both in terms of its capacity and its actions, and the guidance it receives, which directs and applies its desires to the chosen objectives.

3. Often, the will neither desires nor accomplishes what it is capable of desiring and doing due to hindrances. These hindrances can arise from the mind, which misguides the will, or from the work of Satan. As evidenced in the writings of Paul, Satan hin-

dered him from visiting Thessalonica [1 Thessalonians 2:18].

The application of this doctrine serves a twofold purpose. First, the liberty of the will, or rather the misuse of it, becomes the condemnation of the world. In both civil and ecclesiastical matters, individuals fail to exercise their full potential. Even apart from striving for what the Gospel requires, many do not even fulfill what nature itself makes possible. Some may argue that if they are predestined for salvation, they will be saved, and if not, they will not. Consequently, they claim to leave everything to God and live as they please. However, this perspective shall be their condemnation, as they have not lived in accordance with civil virtues, which they could have practiced. They abstain from attending church, neglect the Scriptures, and refrain from hearing sermons. In short, they do not utilize the means of salvation to the extent that their natural strength allows.

Secondly, the weakness of the will within its liberty ought to lead us to humble ourselves and abandon our pride. We must recognize that we cannot perform any action, not even the movement of a hand, foot, or finger, without the assistance of God. Just as Jeroboam found himself unable to retract his outstretched hand after attempting to seize a prophet [1 Kings 13:4], we too are utterly dependent on God for our every action. Such contemplation should also inspire gratitude towards God for enabling us to perform the deeds we do.

The next aspect to consider in the corrupted will is the possibility of desiring what is good. This possibility represents a specific condition of the will, which arises after God has preceded us with His grace. Neither a stone nor a beast possesses this capability because they lack reason and will, rendering them incapable of receiving grace. However, human beings, endowed with both reason and will, possess the potential to perform what they cannot naturally achieve. In this context, the Church fathers often declare, "To have the capacity for faith is natural; to possess faith itself is a matter of grace."

Up to this point, we have explored what the will can accomplish in the corrupted state of humanity. Now, let us delve into what it cannot achieve. This distinction is pivotal and serves as the basis for key differences between our perspective and that of the Church of Rome. I will first establish a solid foundation and subsequently build upon it. The foundational principle is as follows: although the liberty of nature endures, the liberty of grace – the ability to will what is good – is forfeited, extinguished, and eradicated due to Adam's fall. The proof is as follows: the foundation of the liberty of grace lies in the goodness and integrity of the will. However, this goodness and integrity of the will were obliterated by Adam's fall, thus affecting the liberty built upon them. To confirm the loss of this goodness and integrity, consider the following: what we attain in our conversion is what we lack by nature. In our conversion, we assume this goodness as we put on the new man, created according to the image of God in justice and holiness, as articulated by Paul. Furthermore, if every inclination of the heart is persistently and entirely evil, as asserted in Scripture, then no goodness can reside within the heart. Indeed, the Lord observed that "every intent of the thoughts of [man's] heart was only evil continually" [Genesis 6:5]. According to Paul, humanity comprises three components in its state of innocence: the body, the soul, and the spirit – the latter representing the image of God, which is formed by the Spirit and serves as the ornament and glory of the former two. However, following the fall, the spirit degenerates into flesh. As Christ expressed, "That which is born of the flesh is flesh" [John 3:6], signifying complete and exclusive carnality. The natural inclination of the flesh is to lust against the spirit. In light of these considerations, what goodness can possibly exist in the will? The requirement for entering the kingdom of heaven remains consistent with the concept of rebirth. Just as in the initial birth, an imperfect entity is not transformed into a perfect one;

instead, that which was not human is made human. Similarly, in the second birth, the sinner – possessing nothing within to please God – is rendered just and righteous. Regeneration does not pertain to the substance of the body or soul, nor does it involve the faculties of the soul. It solely addresses the goodness of the soul, which aligns with the will of God. Should any portion of this goodness still linger, a new birth cannot occur; only a restoration and reinforcement can take place.

The second rationale for our consideration lies in the absence of an inherent predisposition in a corrupted will to desire what is truly good. Consequently, the liberty of grace to will good is forfeited. Allow me to substantiate this claim further: "A new heart also will I give you, and a new spirit will I put within you and I will take away the stony heart of your body, and I will give you a heart of flesh" [Ezekiel 36:26]. Here, two distinct facets are delineated. Firstly, the new and fleshy heart is a divine gift – a heart that is prepared and inclined to obey. Secondly, within us, there exists no inherent predisposition or capability to accept this divine gift because our hearts are stony. Therefore, God bestows both the fleshy heart and the readiness to accept this gift by removing the stony heart. Christ himself affirms that none can come to Him unless the Father "draws him." If there were even the slightest natural inclination or readiness within us to approach Christ, then such drawing would be unnecessary, as it would indicate obstinate rebellion. Saint Paul contends that the "wisdom of the flesh," signifying the best inclinations and thoughts of the mind of a natural person, are not merely antagonistic, but represent enmity towards God [Romans 8:7]. In enmity, there exists nothing but hatred and contempt for God. Hence, within the context of hatred towards God, what inclination or readiness could there possibly be to love and obey Him? Furthermore, Paul asserts that the natural person "is not capable of the things of God; for they are foolishness to him: neither can he know them, for they are spiritually discerned" [1 Corinthians 2:14]. Within the mind of a natural person, we must consider two elements: the act and the ability to recognize and endorse what is genuinely good. Here, Paul proclaims his stance on both aspects. Regarding the act, he asserts that the mind cannot comprehend the things of God. Concerning the ability, he states that the mind lacks the capacity or predisposition to acknowledge or endorse them, comparing it to a small vessel incapable of containing a large quantity of liquid. Additionally, Paul reminds us that we are "inadequate or insufficient of ourselves" [2 Corinthians 3:5] to even conceive a virtuous thought independently. Our sufficiency, instead, comes from God. Thus, nature, tainted by corruption, lacks the ability even to conceive a virtuous thought, let alone the desire for what is truly good. Paul also informs the Ephesians that they were once "dead in sins and trespasses" [Ephesians 2:1]. This spiritual deadness does not solely pertain to the performance of good deeds but also encompasses the ability to enact them. If even the slightest capacity for good remained after the fall, humanity would not yet be considered dead but rather approaching death or deterioration, as some vestige of spiritual life would still linger. If this were true, how could we be "quickened together with Christ" [Ephesians 2:5]? Furthermore, how could it be considered a wonder that the "dead hear the voice of Christ" [John 5:25]? Paul also addresses the Ephesians, proclaiming that they were "once darkness" [Ephesians 5:8], a state devoid of any readiness to either emit or receive light. Yet, they were transformed without any effort or cooperation on their part, much like light emerged from darkness during creation [2 Corinthians 4:6].

The third rationale stems from our not merely being impotent for goodness but, rather, possessing an overwhelming propensity and inclination towards evil, rendering us incapable of anything but sin. Jeremiah poignantly declares, "The heart of man is wicked above all things" [Jeremiah 17:9], leaving us to ponder, "Who can truly comprehend it?" The apostle Paul, in addressing the Romans, once characterized them as "slaves to sin, free in terms of righteousness" [Romans 6:20]. Paul himself, acknowledging the spiritual nature of the law, candidly admits that he is "carnal and enslaved by sin" [Romans 7:14]. Regarding those unrepentant, Paul asserts that they find themselves ensnared by the devil, succumbing to his will [2 Timothy 2:26]. It is vital to emphasize that this disposition encompasses not just a few sins but extends to all sins without exception. Just as every individual inherits the entirety of human nature from Adam, so too does one inherit the complete corruption of human nature. In the presence of this vast and dreadful corruption, any inclination or capacity for goodness must inevitably yield. An objection may arise, contending that if the will is enslaved by sin, it has wholly lost its freedom. To this, I respond by drawing an analogy to a prisoner: even though a prisoner may have lost a substantial portion of their freedom, they have not forfeited it entirely. Within the confines of their cell, they may still choose to sit, stand, lie down, or walk. Likewise, one who is enslaved to sin may be limited to sinning, but within that scope, they retain the freedom to exercise their will in various forms of wickedness, thus illustrating the paradoxical nature of human will.

The fourth rationale reinforces the idea that all goodness attributed to us, as well as any pleasing actions before God, is unequivocally ascribed to God in Scripture. Those who are children of God are born of God, a birth not attributed to blood (natural generation), the will of the flesh (the power and inclination of natural will), or the will of man (the heroic inclination of exceptional individuals) [John 1:13]. We are considered God's handiwork, created in Christ for good works [Ephesians 2:10]. It is paramount to recognize that the created being contributes nothing to their own creation; creation is a process where something emerges from nothing. As Christ asserts, "Without me, you can do nothing." The rationale behind this statement lies in the analogy of Christ being the vine and believers being its branches. These branches, in order to bear good fruit, must first be engrafted into Christ and subsequently draw their nourishment – their ability to perform good – from Him.

Advocates for the inherent freedom of the human will in moral actions, opposing the doctrine of grace, present four specific arguments. The first argument posits that God has issued numerous commandments to humanity post-fall, encompassing both moral and gospel commandments, such as the command to turn to God, believe, and repent. These commandments, it is argued, would be in vain if there were no freedom of will to either obey or disobey them. To this, I respond initially by clarifying that these commandments do not dictate what we are capable of doing but rather what we ought to do. They signify not our ability but our duty and responsibility to please God and attain salvation. Moreover, if these commandments appear impossible to fulfill, the fault lies not with God but with our corrupted nature. Secondly, even though we may lack the will to carry out what God commands, His commandments are not futile. They serve as instruments and means through which the Spirit of God accomplishes the good that He commands within us.

The second objection contends that we are obligated to give an account of all our actions on the day of judgment, and this requirement would not be equitable unless we possessed the power to will both good and evil. In response, I affirm that the obligation to give an account arises from our previous possession of the liberty to will either good or evil in Adam. All individuals, post-fall, retain a degree of free will: the wicked exercise it in sin, while the righteous exercise it in acts of righteousness.

The third objection is rooted in scriptural references. It is argued that the wounded Samaritan lying between Jericho and Jerusalem [Luke 10:30] symbolizes humanity, half-dead in sin. I clarify that parables should not be used to derive teachings beyond their intended scope. In this parable, the primary purpose is to elucidate the concept of one's neighbor. We concede that the freedom of the will is not obliterated but rather wounded. Although liberty of grace to will good is forfeited, the natural liberty to will still persists. Additionally, objections are raised regarding the words of Christ to the angel of Laodicea: "Behold I stand at the door and knock: if any man open, I will come in" [Revelation 3:20]. Some argue that "knocking" represents the work of grace, while "opening" signifies the act of free will. In response, I note that the phrase "if any man open" is conditional and thus does not definitively establish the scope of the will's power. Furthermore, these words do not describe what the angel can do but rather emphasize his role and what he can accomplish through grace.

Another scriptural reference cited is from Deuteronomy: "The word which I command thee, is near thee, that thou mayst do it" [Deuteronomy 30:14]. In this context, Moses is elucidating what the Israelites can do through the grace of a mediator—One who fulfills the law on their behalf and provides the grace required for obedience. Through this perspective, Paul interprets this text (Romans 10:8), emphasizing that the statements of the law should be understood not in a legalistic but an evangelical manner, specifically for those in Christ who fulfill the law through Him.

The fourth objection posits that when a person is converted, it is not against their will; otherwise, God would treat them as if they were a stone or a beast. Therefore, it is argued that conversion occurs with the individual's consent of their own will. In response, it is important to understand that this consent originates not from ourselves but from God. Just as the act of conversion is the work of God, so too is the will to be converted. This point will be further elaborated upon later.

Based on the previously established foundation, we can address several significant questions. The first question is whether a natural person or an unbeliever, without faith and without the aid of God, can perform any morally good work—namely, an action devoid of sin. The Church of Rome has asserted for many centuries that, even without faith, a person, without being tempted, can, with the special help of God, perform morally good deeds, free from sin. However, we respond with a resounding "no," and this assertion is supported by ample evidence.

The beginning of an action is reflective of the nature of the action itself. The human mind and will serve as the origins of all actions, and within them, there exists no capability to think or will that which is truly good. Instead, there persists a continual inclination towards the contrary. Consequently, all actions emanating from this source are perpetually tainted by evil. In accordance with this doctrine, Paul declares that everything is unclean, and the use of all things is unclean. Christ affirms that an "evil tree cannot bring forth good fruit," and Scripture unequivocally states, "Whatsoever is not of faith is sin." The orthodox and ancient church has consistently subscribed to this doctrine. The Ararsican Council attests that it is God's gift that keeps us from injustice and that "all we can do is God's." Jerome asserts that "without Christ every virtue is but a vice," and Gregory emphasizes that "if faith be not first wrought in our heart, other things cannot be good, though they seem to be so." Augustine explicitly maintains that "all the works of unbelievers are sins, because whatever is not of faith is sin." He goes on to express that Pelagius, the heretic, sometimes balanced the power of the will with such precision that he suggested it had some influence in preventing sin, which, according to Augustine, leaves no room for the help of grace, without which free will is entirely powerless in preventing sin. Augustine's statement reveals two significant points. First, that free will, in his view, is inherently incapable of preventing sin. Second, it was considered heretical by Augustine for Pelagius to suggest that free will could partially prevent sin through its own capacity. The Council of Trent's anathema against anyone claiming that all works performed before justification are indeed sins further underscores this belief. This anathema indirectly implies that, prior to the grace of justification, the will can partially assist and act morally good, as the Church of Rome often argues. To evade this charge, they respond by asserting that Pelagius intended to convey that the will has the power to prevent sin throughout a person's entire life. However, Augustine's response clearly demonstrates that Pelagius's intention extended to individual actions, as evidenced by the phrase: "He that prays, 'Lead us not into temptation,' prays that he may not do any evil." Vincentius Lyrinensis also identifies Pelagianism as the belief that free will possesses such great virtue that the grace of God is not deemed necessary to assist it in performing good deeds in every single act. This view, as expressed by Vincentius, was unprecedented before the advent of Pelagius.

Contrary arguments suggest that infidels can perform good deeds according to the law, and that they possess various virtues as gifts from God. In response, it must be understood that while infidels may engage in actions that are outwardly good, their intentions are often misguided. They pursue these deeds for self-serving purposes, such as honor, profit, or pleasure. When a good action is undertaken with the wrong motives, it loses its inherent goodness and becomes tainted by the intentions of the doer. Moreover, the virtues found in the lives of non-believers, as they originate from God, are indeed good. However, when these virtues are misused or, more accurately, abused by individuals, they can lead to sinful outcomes.

Another objection arises concerning the biblical account of Pharaoh, who, in a moment of desperation, confessed, "I have sinned, the Lord is righteous, I and my people are sinners: pray for me," etc. This confession, while possessing a certain goodness in its form, does not indicate true goodness in Pharaoh himself. His words were not born out of love for God but rather stemmed from a fear of impending punishment. Additionally, Pharaoh's confession was insincere, as he later hardened his heart, demonstrating his lack of genuine repentance.

Furthermore, it is argued that Nebuchadnezzar, a pagan ruler, received a reward from God for his conquest of Tyre [Ezek. 29:20]. It is asserted that God would not have rewarded him if his actions were sinful.

In response, it should be noted that Nebuchadnezzar's reward was of a temporal nature and pertained solely to his labor. This reward did not reflect the inherent goodness of his actions.

Lastly, one might contend that if we are incapable of performing good works due to our corrupt will, then all our actions—such as eating, drinking, sleeping, buying, selling, and everything we engage in—are sinful. This could lead to the belief that nothing should be done at all. However, actions such as these, which are part of human life, are not inherently sinful. Their moral character is determined by the manner in which they are performed. These actions become sinful when they are not carried out in obedience to God and when they lack a proper reference to Him as their ultimate purpose. It is important to recognize that until a person experiences a transformation through grace, their actions are tainted by sin even when they appear virtuous in the eyes of others.

This understanding of the doctrine serves as a corrective to the misconception held by many individuals. They may believe themselves to be in a state of favor with God simply because they refrain from heinous crimes such as theft, murder, blasphemy, or adultery. However, they are mistaken. Everyone possesses within themselves enough grounds for condemnation because all their actions are sinful in the sight of God until they undergo renewal through His grace. Even seemingly mundane activities like eating, drinking, sleeping, buying, and selling can be sinful when not carried out with the right motives and in obedience to God's will.

Secondly, we are taught that, until we experience spiritual rebirth, our lives are marked by a persistent inclination towards sin and our subjugation to the influence of sin and Satan. It is crucial for us to recognize and acknowledge this bondage, allowing ourselves to truly feel its weight, and even groaning under its burden. Once we have done this, we must take another step forward, approaching the Mediator, Christ, with hearts filled with hunger and thirst. Christ, who proclaims liberation to those held captive, offers deliverance from the clutches of sin, Satan, hell, death, and condemnation to all who, with contrite and wounded hearts, seek refuge in Him.

Moving to the second question, it inquires whether a natural person, through the strength of their will, can resist and overcome temptation. The papal perspective suggests that individuals can overcome smaller and easier temptations on their own and can also triumph over greater temptations with God's assistance. According to this view, various temptations do not surpass the natural strength of human beings. However, our position and teaching assert the opposite. We maintain that, following Adam's fall, the human will lacks the capacity to conquer even the slightest temptation. This deficiency stems from the loss and annihilation of the ability to reject evil and choose good. Without the power to resist, genuine resistance cannot occur. In our prayers to God, when we entreat Him saying, "Lead us not into temptation," we acknowledge that, without God's assistance, there is no temptation that we can withstand by our own strength. In urging us to "resist Satan, our adversary," Peter prescribes the appropriate means, emphasizing the importance of standing firm in faith.

An objection arises, suggesting that a natural person can either sin or abstain from sin. This assertion holds true concerning actions related to external conduct and visible sins, such as murder, theft, or adultery. Yet, it is not universally true, but applicable only at certain times. Even the righteous occasionally stumble into overt transgressions. Moreover, when a natural person refrains from committing blatant sins, it does not signify victory. This restraint from outward sinful acts does not eliminate the wicked inclinations of the heart. Furthermore, this abstinence from visible sin is not without sin itself because it arises from a heart that remains unreconciled with God. It does not originate from a foundation of faith but rather for self-serving reasons, such as seeking praise, avoiding public shame, and not for the honor and glory of God.

The third question pertains to whether an unregenerate person, through the power of their will, can obey the law, at least in terms of the core action. Throughout history, a prevalent belief in schools and churches has been that they can indeed do so. It was thought that, for a brief period, one could keep all the moral commandments, preventing any sin from occurring. However, the reality is quite different. An unregenerate individual cannot achieve this feat because the very foundation and origin of their capacity to choose what is good has been lost. Consequently, there can be no adherence to the law in terms of its core substance. The essence of the first set of commandments involves loving God with all one's heart, soul, and strength, while the essence of all negative commands is encapsulated in "You shall not covet." These lofty requirements exceed the natural capacity of the will. Some may argue that an unregenerate person can still perform acts of charity, uphold justice, and the like. To this, I respond that within any commanded duty, two essential components exist: the actual deed to be performed and the manner in which it is executed. The latter involves carrying out the task in faith, with the intent to obey God and honor Him through it. This manner of fulfilling a duty constitutes the essence of every good work, and without it, the works prescribed by the law are like lifeless bodies, lacking a soul or form. Consequently, the will is incapable of upholding any commandment in its entirety.

Furthermore, it is essential to emphasize that the law not only demands external actions but also requires internal obedience. This internal obedience includes knowledge of God and His will, faith, hope, love, patience, and the subjugation of our thoughts, desires, and affections to God's will. Concerning this internal and spiritual obedience, the Holy Spirit declares that the law is impossible to fulfill (Romans 8:3). It is stated that the wisdom of the flesh cannot submit to God's law (v. 7) and that this burden is one neither we nor our forefathers could bear (Acts 15:10).

It is worth noting that Pelagius propagated the heretical notion that an individual, through the sheer strength of their free will, could uphold all of God's commandments, even if it required considerable effort. The papal position is not far from this, suggesting that, by natural strength, one may observe the entire law for a brief period. However, these ideas are fundamentally flawed and contrary to the truth of human nature and the requirements of God's law.

The fourth question addresses whether the corrupted will of a natural person can, in any way, prepare and arrange itself for its own conversion and justification. This entails removing hindrances and rendering oneself suitable and capable of justification. For many centuries, the prevailing doctrine asserted that the will possessed this capability, and even today, the belief among papists is that the will, if moved by God, can accomplish this. However, the undeniable truth is that the will cannot achieve this on its own. The conversion of a sinner is an act of creation, and no created being can self-prepare for its own creation. The very means by which a person might prepare themselves for any righteous act was forfeited due to Adam's fall. Therefore, the work of preparation belongs to God, not us, unless one can imagine a spiritually dead person preparing themselves for their own spiritual justification. By our natural state, we are enslaved to sin, and our freedom begins with our justification. Thus, before we are justified, we lack the capacity even to will that which is good. It is true that the Israelites "prepared their hearts to seek the Lord" (1 Samuel 7:2), and Ezra "prepared his heart to seek the law of the Lord" (Ezra 7:10). However, this was the labor of those who had been regenerated, renewing their commitment to obey God and persevere in acts of godliness.

The fifth and most crucial question of all pertains to whether a natural person can, of their own will, desire their own conversion or regeneration. The scholars among the papists teach the following: that will alone, by itself, cannot accomplish this, but that the will can, if it is prompted and stirred by some good thoughts placed in the mind and some good desires kindled in the heart, and if it is also aided and guided by God. They illustrate this concept with the following comparisons: In darkness, the eye sees nothing and seems incapable of sight. Yet, when an object is presented before the eye and light is introduced, it can then perceive. Similarly, a person may slumber in a dark cell, not even contemplating escape. However, if someone calls to him, extends a rope, and he awakens to seize it, as Jeremiah did, he will hold on and emerge from the dungeon. In this view, both the ability to will and the execution of conversion are attributed to the individual, albeit with divine assistance.

Contrarily, the doctrine we espouse asserts the opposite: the will, before being turned and converted, cannot even will its own conversion. This conclusion stems from the preceding argument: the power to will that which is truly good is lost. A power to will our conversion is, by nature, a power to will what is good. Therefore, the power to will our own conversion is also forfeited. Beyond the prompting and stirring of motions that assist the will, what is further needed is that the will be regenerated before it can truly will what is good. Without this gift of regeneration, which constitutes the authentic prevenient grace, all external influences and incitements towards what is good are rendered ineffectual. The cause must precede the effect. To effect and perform what is good, the initial cause is the regeneration of the will, which provides the will with not only a new action by which it desires what is good but also a new quality by which it becomes capable of willing what is good. This capability to will what is good precedes the actual act of willing, just as the cause precedes the effect. When a person is dead, you may rub and massage them, even warm their heart with spirits. However, without the soul being restored to the body, all efforts are in vain. Similarly, no persuasive argument directed at the mind or good desires within the will hold any significance until the image of God, representing holiness and conformity with God's will, begins to be restored within. In fact, the mind cannot generate a good thought, and the will cannot hold a good desire until God renews them with a new quality or characteristic of holiness. This enables the mind to think well and the will to desire well, or, in other words, to will what is good. Although the will possesses the natural inclination to will or not, the ability and formal commencement of willing what is good is dependent on the integrity or goodness of the will. To conclude, although the will by its nature possesses the inclination to will or not, the ability to begin willing what is good is a result of the integrity or goodness of the will, bestowed by God. It is objected that the will to accept and receive grace is within us before grace is received. I reply as follows: the initial act of the will, whereby it, in its regeneration, starts to assent to God and begins to will to be converted, indeed emanates from the will (because the will does the willing). Nevertheless, it does not originate from the natural capacity of the will but from the grace of God that renews it. For the will to will its own regeneration is the consequence and indication of the initiated regeneration. In handling the topic of a sinner's predestination and justification, Paul likens God to a potter and us to clay. The clay, prior to being molded into a vessel of honor and during its shaping, remains entirely passive and does not contribute to its own shaping. When a person is to be regenerated, God removes the stony heart that, by nature, disobeys and is wholly unfit for obedience. In its place, God imparts a fleshy heart, malleable and receptive to obedience. To will to be converted is a virtuous act and a form of genuine obedience; therefore, it does not emerge from a person's heart until it has been softened and shaped by God toward what is good. The Apostle Paul says, "What do you have that you did not receive? If then you received it, why do you boast as if you did not receive it?" (1 Corinthians 4:7). If to will to be healed were from us, we would have reason to boast in ourselves. He also proclaims that we are not capable of thinking a good thought by our own volition but that our sufficiency comes from God. Consequently, it is even less plausible that, of our own accord, we would will or desire our own regeneration. The spiritual health and life of the soul come from God, who raises us from death to life. To will to be healed and to will to live for God is the initial stage of recovery and life. A certain council declared, "If anyone claims that God anticipates our will so that it may be purified from sin and does not acknowledge that it is the operation of the Spirit of God within us that makes us will to be purified, he resists the Holy Spirit, thus contradicting Solomon's statement, 'The will is prepared by God.'" Augustine affirms, "It is not in him who runs, but in God who shows mercy, so that all may be ascribed to God, who both prepares the will of man for help and assists the will that has been prepared, for it is not in vain." People who are physically ill can desire to be healed before their healing process begins because they are alive. However, those who are spiritually sick in sin are dead in their sins before their conversion. Consequently, they are incapable of thinking, willing, or desiring their own conversion. When Christ was about to heal a sick man, He posed this question, "Do you want to be healed?" (John 5:6). Similarly, when God initiates the work of regeneration in a person, He internally raises the question in their heart about whether they desire to be regenerated, thereby stirring up a desire for regeneration. If anyone fears that this doctrine implies that individuals are regenerated against their will, I respond that when God commences our regeneration, He also makes us willing participants, as opposed to forcing us against our wills. Therefore, regeneration occurs not against our wills but with the will being rendered willing, though this willingness originates not from us but from God. To clarify this doctrine further, I will introduce two additional questions.

The first question pertains to whether the natural strength of man's will plays any role in his own conversion. The papist response posits that the will, in conjunction with the grace of God, contributes to our conversion—grace being the principal cause, and the will a secondary cause, with both serving as formal causes. However, our position, based on the truth, maintains that the will, when engaged in the act of bringing about conversion or regeneration, does not act as a cause at all. Rather, in its essence, the will is merely a recipient or subject, open to receiving the grace of conversion imparted and wrought by God. It is illogical to propose that a creature could be the cause of its own creation or that a dead person could bring about their own revival. Thus, the doctrine of those who contend that there are three efficient causes of man's conversion—God's Spirit, God's Word, and man's will—reveals a deficiency. The Spirit stands as the primary cause, the Word, when employed correctly, serves as the means or instrument through which the Spirit's operation becomes effective, and human will remains solely as the object of divine operation.

It may be argued that individuals who repent are worthy of praise, and this can only be the case if repentance stems from the freedom of the will. I respond as follows: repentance merits praise because it is something that pleases God and, in that sense, is commendable. However, a repentant person is not praised because they are the cause of their own repentance but because they repent, enabled by the mercy of God.

The second question pertains to whether the conversion of a sinner is, in any way, within the power of human will. The papist answer posits that our regeneration and conversion partially lie within the power of the human will. In this view, the will, when stirred, can either incline towards God's grace or reject it. In contrast, we teach that regeneration is not subject to the power of human will; rather, it entirely depends on God's will. When God intends to convert and renew us, although the will, by its nature, is prone to resist, it cannot resist or thwart God's work due to God's unchanging will and the effectiveness of His inner operation. For when God Himself undertakes any task, His work is impervious to resistance. His work simply consists of willing it into existence, and His will cannot be opposed. In the process of human conversion, He operates on both the will and the deed, causing people to follow His commandments. Therefore, resistance is futile. Moreover, Scripture consistently conveys that our conversion and salvation are wholly dependent on God's will and not on human will. In addressing the distinction among individuals concerning salvation, Paul cites Moses: "It does not depend on the one who wills or the one who runs, but on God who has mercy" (Romans 9:16). Jesus Himself teaches that the mysteries of the kingdom of God are revealed to some and hidden from others "because it is the Father's good pleasure" (Matthew 11:26), and because understanding is granted to some but withheld from others (Luke 8:10). Our conversion is described as a "new birth" and a "new creation." Therefore, it cannot be subject to human will, for a created being has no say in its own creation or regeneration, as it cannot choose to accept or reject it. The idea that the possession or absence of grace depends on the choice of human will undermines the grace of God.

An objection to this doctrine arises from instances where individuals resisted God's will for their conversion, such as in the case of Jerusalem. I respond by distinguishing between two types of divine work. The first is external, occurring through the Word and sacraments, where God offers grace, and indeed, this can be resisted. This is what Christ speaks of when He says, "They were not willing," and Stephen when he declares that "they resisted the Holy Spirit" (Acts 7:51). The Lord stated in Genesis 6:3, "My Spirit shall not strive with man forever," and Peter attributes this striving to Noah's ministry, saying that "Christ went and preached to the spirits in prison" (1 Peter 3:19). The second type of divine work is inward, where God, through His Spirit, transforms, renews, and sanctifies the entire person. This work is impervious to the resistance of human will, just as Lazarus could not resist Christ's act of raising him from the dead. If it is argued that this doctrine negates human freedom because it negates the ability to choose or reject God's grace, I respond with this: the angels of God, who desire only what is good and cannot desire evil, possess perfect freedom of will. It is a greater expression of freedom to desire solely what is good than to have the ability to choose both good and evil. True freedom lies in desiring only what God wills and nothing else. In summary, based on everything presented, it is evident that the difference between our perspective and that of the Church of Rome on the matter of free will centers on the assertion that the freedom of the will to choose what is good is either weakened or merely constrained by sin, whereas we believe it is entirely lost and nullified by Adam's fall.

Furthermore, the previous doctrine provides a straightforward response to a common question: where does the effectiveness of God's grace reside? Some within the papist tradition assert that it ordinarily resides in the free consent and cooperation of the will, combined with grace. This perspective appears to align with the views of the Council of Trent. However, attributing the efficacy of divine grace to human will diminishes the divine nature of God's grace and can foster human pride. Others suggest that grace's effectiveness lies in the suitability of the persuasive message—essentially, in moral persuasion. They believe that God knows how to craft messages that are apt and convincing, similar to how a beast is moved by the sight of food. Yet, these persuasions have no real efficacy in moving the will because it remains in bondage under sin and Satan. The will not only needs assistance but must also be liberated from this bondage before any persuasive messages can sway it. Lombard, from an earlier time, deviated somewhat from the purity of the past, but even he holds a sounder view than the Jesuits of our day. He acknowledges that "free will is now hindered by the law of the flesh from doing good and is incited to evil, to the point where it cannot will and do good unless delivered and aided by grace." Departing from the Papists in their disagreements, we place the efficacy of grace in grace itself. As Christ says, "Everyone who has heard and learned from the Father comes to me." Additionally, we see that God supplements the first grace with a second. After granting the power, He does not stop there but goes further, offering the will, and along with the will, the action. It is in this way that the grace of God is effective.

The contemplation and application of these preceding doctrines bear great significance. Firstly, if the liberty of grace is indeed lost, the need for our redemption by Christ is paramount, highlighting its profound excellence. Secondly, this doctrine removes any excuse for sin because, although we sin out of necessity due to the loss of liberty of grace, we still sin voluntarily, maintaining our freedom in choosing evil. Thirdly, it underscores that any goodness man possesses or retains is solely a result of what God gives and sustains within us. This should compel us to fervently pray for the grace we lack and to offer heartfelt gratitude for the graces we receive. Fourthly, we are compelled to humble ourselves deeply, recognizing the loss of our liberty and our bondage under sin, and to pray fervently for deliverance through Christ. Fifthly, since we cannot, on our own, overcome even the smallest temptation, we must continuously seek God's guidance and assistance through prayer. Lastly, understanding that our conversion depends on God's mercy and not on our will, we are led to renounce our own desires, wisdom, and power, attributing our justification and salvation wholly and exclusively to God.

The third state of man is the state of regeneration, wherein the will possesses the power to desire both what is good and what is evil, as daily life illustrates in the conduct of righteous individuals. The reason for this is that the renewed will of man encompasses three types of liberty. The first is the natural liberty to choose or reject, which is inherent in all humans. The second is the liberty of sin, through which the will, when choosing evil, does so willingly. This liberty diminishes in proportion to the measure of grace bestowed by God. The third is the liberty of grace, allowing the will to desire what pleases God. This is partially restored during regeneration, to the extent that the liberty to sin is diminished.

Because these three forms of liberty persist in the will until death, it alternates between willing what is good and what is evil, and sometimes, both. Even in our best actions, there is a mixture because, during this earthly life, they are not entirely good but rather partly good and partly tainted by evil.

To better understand the power of the will, let us explore four key questions. The first question pertains to whether the will, whether prevented or renewed, plays a role in the initial regeneration of a sinner. In response, we must consider two aspects of a sinner's transformation. First, there is the inception or foundation, which involves the implantation of new qualities and inclinations within the mind, will, and affections of the heart. In this regard, the entire process is solely and wholly the work of God upon us and within us. We are passive recipients, not active participants.

The second aspect involves the manifestation of these newfound qualities through new and spiritual actions, such as thinking, willing, and choosing what is good. These actions are the result of God's work within and through the human will. The will is not just a recipient but also an instrument: it is subject to God's work, as He is the primary agent behind these actions, yet it also functions as an instrument that God employs to accomplish His purposes. Thus, the will is not purely passive but rather both passive and active, albeit sequentially. Initially, it is passive as it is acted upon and moved by God, who initiates both the will and the deed. Later, it becomes active, functioning in response to God's grace.

It is important to note that we do not entirely deny the cooperation of the human will with God's grace. God's primary role is to regenerate us, making us His children and new creations. In this process, we do not cooperate with God but act as recipients, allowing God to work in us and reform us, much like when He initially created us without our assistance. However, after our regeneration, faith brings us from spiritual death to life, and we find that the will is present within us, albeit to a limited extent due to the remnants of corruption. At this point, we begin to collaborate with the grace of God. Moved by God's grace, we are inclined to will what is good, and indeed, we actively will what is good. In this sense, it has been wisely stated that what is being restored within us is not restored without our involvement. God, in those whom He calls, prepares the will to be a receptive vessel and a servant of His gifts.

Let me present the same answer in a different manner. In the process of our regeneration, we can identify three distinct graces: preventing grace, working grace, and coworking grace. Preventing grace occurs when, in His mercy, God instills a new light in our minds, a new quality or inclination in our wills, and new affections in our hearts. Working grace is when God enables our will to engage in virtuous acts, such as the will to believe, the will to repent, and the will to obey God's word. Coworking grace, on the other hand, involves God enabling our will to carry out these virtuous deeds. Preventing grace provides the power for good, working grace bestows the will, and coworking grace empowers the deed. Together, these three graces constitute the work of regeneration.

In the realm of preventing grace, the human will does not actively cooperate but remains passive, like a vessel ready to receive grace. This is because it is God's exclusive role to establish new faculties and inclinations within the will. However, after the will has been renewed and is receptive to God's grace, it begins to actively cooperate with God's working and coworking grace. In this stage, the will, moved by God's grace, willingly and actively engages in virtuous acts. The will acts and moves because it has been set in motion by God's grace, becoming both a subject and an instrument for God's work.

It is crucial to understand that we do not entirely deny the cooperation of the human will with God's grace. God's primary action is to regenerate us, making us His children and new creations, during which we do not cooperate but merely receive His work. However, after our regeneration, faith ushers us from spiritual death to life, and the will is present within us, albeit to a limited extent due to remaining corruption. At this point, we begin to collaborate with God's grace. Moved by His grace, we willingly engage in virtuous acts such as believing and obeying. In this sense, the ancient saying holds true: "He who made you without you does not regenerate or save you without you." This signifies that our conversion does not occur without the motion and consent of the will, unlike our initial creation.

To further grasp this concept, we must remember the order between the human will and God's grace. In terms of time, they occur simultaneously, working together from the very moment of our regeneration. However, in terms of the natural order, the will does not initiate what is good and then seek assistance from grace. Instead, grace precedes, renews, and moves the will. Subsequently, the will, having been transformed or influenced by God, desires to be converted and healed in the initial instant of conversion.

This operation of the will to believe, to repent, and to obey is a minimal expression of God's favor. While it may seem insignificant to merely will to do good, it holds great value because it carries God's promise. For example, the prophet Isaiah calls upon the rebellious Israelites to wash and make themselves clean, to cease from evil, and to learn to do good. Yet, recognizing their inability, he reassures them that if they earnestly will to be cleansed and demonstrate this will through their efforts to obey, they will partake in the goodness of the land.

Similarly, Christ assures us that the heavenly Father grants the Holy Spirit to those who desire Him. Furthermore, God accepts this act of willing goodness as if it were the actual deed itself. Therefore, the beginning of faith and conversion, even if it is feeble, yet genuine, is pleasing to God. Nevertheless, our inclination toward faith and conversion is only possible through the unique mercy of God, who stirs the hearts of the elect by His Holy Spirit. In this context, Christ's words in Matthew 11:30, "My yoke is easy, and my burden is light," hold profound significance. Likewise, John emphasizes that God's commandments are not burdensome (1 John 5:3).

It may be argued that the will and desire for renewal and reconciliation with God can coexist with a mindset and intent to sin, lacking a genuine hatred and detestation of iniquity. In response, it is essential to recognize that a sincere and fervent will or desire to believe in Christ and to repent inherently includes a deep-seated aversion to sin and a resolute commitment to forsake it. One who genuinely desires to believe does so out of a profound disdain for their unbelief. Similarly, a genuine desire to repent arises from a genuine abhorrence of one's sinful ways, accompanied by a firm resolve to sin no more.

The second question revolves around whether the will, once it has been renewed, possesses the inherent capability to generate and bring forth good works independently. To address this, we must consider two aspects.

Firstly, the will, on its own, lacks the ability to do so without a twofold grace bestowed by God. The first aspect is what we might call "supportive grace," which comprises three essential actions: preservation, confirmation, and protection. Preservation signifies God's continuous sustenance of the renewed will, for even the slightest good within us cannot endure without His upholding hand. Confirmation involves God establishing the mind in righteousness, ensuring that the will steadfastly adheres to virtuous inclinations, as it is otherwise prone to wavering. Protection denotes God's defense of His grace within us against the onslaught of temptation. Recall how Christ told Peter that Satan sought to sift him, but Christ prayed that his faith might not fail. Additionally, God assures us that He will not allow the faithful to face temptations beyond their capacity to withstand.

The second aspect can be referred to as "enabling grace," by which God moves and ignites the will, enabling it to genuinely desire and perform good deeds. This grace is typically required for the accomplishment of any virtuous work. Consider David, whose heart was profoundly renewed by the Holy Spirit, yet he still prayed, "Incline my heart to your testimonies." Similarly, the Christian soul, though already drawn to Christ, fervently prays, "Draw me, and we will run after you." The Apostle Paul informs us that the children of God are led, moved, and stirred by the Spirit of God. Even the Philippians, having undergone renewal and working out their salvation with fear and trembling, experienced God continually working within them. God stirs the will, motivating it to both desire and act upon the good it is capable of. This divine impetus originates from God's benevolent will.

It should not surprise us when I assert that new grace is essential to rouse the will for each new virtuous undertaking. The grace within the will is akin to a fire fueled by green wood, which barely burns and fails to sustain itself unless it is consistently stirred and fanned. In the same vein, the inclination of the will toward good, entwined though it may be with opposing corruption that seeks to deter, tempt, incite, and pull it away from God and righteousness, necessitates perpetual stimulation, agitation, and impetus.

While the regenerated individual possesses the capacity to pray to God, there are moments when they find it challenging due to the weight of inherent corruption. In such instances, the Spirit intervenes, assisting in bearing the burden of human frailty and prompting us to make our requests. The ancient teachings of the church have consistently emphasized the necessity of "new grace being granted for every virtuous act." This underscores the fact that we do not perform the good deeds we are capable of unless God compels us to do so, just as He empowered us with the ability in the first place.

This doctrine deserves our attention, especially in light of differing views within the Catholic tradition, which claim that our wills, aided by grace, can produce good deeds without requiring the additional impetus of new grace to arouse and invigorate the will. Indeed, for natural actions, the general cooperation of God suffices. However, when it comes to the accomplishment of supernatural actions, the specific assistance of God becomes indispensable. Imagine a child capable of walking on a level surface with the support of their mother's hand. Despite this ability, they remain unable to ascend a flight of stairs without being lifted at each step. A similar analogy applies to the children of God in matters pertaining to the kingdom of heaven.

The second aspect to consider is that when the renewed will performs a good deed, it does so imperfectly. As Paul articulates, "I have the desire to do what is good, but I cannot carry it out" [Romans 7:18]. In other words, "I cannot do it perfectly as I would wish." One might raise an objection: God's works are perfect, and good works performed by us are considered works of God; hence, they should be perfect. To this, I respond to the first part of the objection, affirming that it holds true for works accomplished solely by God, as well as for works jointly executed by both God and man, where God serves as the principal agent and man as the instrument. In the latter case, the work bears the imprint of human imperfection, given that it flows through the sinful mind and will of man. Consider a skilled scribe who, on his own, writes with perfect penmanship. However, when he assists a learner who writes alongside him, the result will inevitably carry the imperfections of the learner's skill. Similarly, in all works that emanate from God through us, this principle applies.

The third question pertains to whether the remnants of corruption possess sufficient potency to extinguish the Spirit of God within the renewed will. The response is that, on its own, remaining corruption is indeed inclined to achieve this, and the mutable nature of God's

Spirit makes it susceptible to extinguishment. Nevertheless, it cannot be utterly lost for four reasons. Firstly, the promise of God within the covenant of grace ensures, "I will put my fear into their hearts, that they shall not depart from me" [Jeremiah 32:40]. This promise particularly extends to all genuine believers, as it constitutes a core element of the evangelical covenant. Secondly, Christ's intercession on behalf of all the elect provides an additional safeguard. Christ assured Peter, "Satan has desired to sift you as wheat, but I have prayed for you, Peter, that your faith may not fail" [Luke 22:31]. He made this intercession most notably in the solemn prayer recorded in John 17, where He prayed not only for Peter but for all the apostles and all who would believe in Him. The third reason is the omnipotent power of God, which preserves all those in Christ. Christ himself asserts, "No one can snatch my sheep out of my hand" [John 10:28], underscoring the paramount reason: "My Father is greater than all." The final cause is the efficacy of God's Spirit. According to Saint John, "God's seed remains in those who are born anew," and this seed "preserves them, preventing them from willingly sinning in two ways" [Romans 7:19]. First, if they do sin, it is not with full consent of their will. They harbor a partial aversion to the evil they commit. Second, if they stumble due to human frailty, they do not persist in sin or maintain a course of wickedness. Instead, the remaining seed of grace prompts them to return to God and seek restoration through renewed repentance.

The last question inquires whether the renewed will can persevere in doing good on its own accord. To this, I respond that our perseverance hinges solely upon the will of God. Two elements are essential for our perseverance: the ability to persevere and the will to persevere. Both of these, being inherently good, emanate from God. As the Scriptures affirm, "Every good and perfect gift is from above, coming down from the Father of the heavenly lights" [James 4:17].

This initial teaching holds great significance. It reminds us that the rebirth and regeneration of a sinner do not occur without the movement of their own will. Thus, we are instructed that if we earnestly desire our own salvation, we must employ the means of grace, contend against our inner struggles, and wholeheartedly strive by seeking, asking, and knocking. Some may argue that faith, repentance, and other virtues are all divine gifts. To this, I respond that there is no virtue or divine gift within us that does not involve our wills. In every virtuous act, God's grace and the will of man collaborate—God's grace as the primary cause and the renewed will of man as the instrument of God. Therefore, diligence, effort, and prayer on our part are necessary in all matters of virtue and righteousness.

Furthermore, this doctrine brings genuine solace to all devoted servants of God. When they employ the means of salvation, such as the Word, prayer, and sacraments, and their wills begin to resist unbelief and other sinful inclinations, simply desiring to believe, repent, and turn to God, they have initiated their return to God. God, in turn, has commenced the process of regeneration in them. Provided their willingness is sincere and earnest, they should nurture this small spark until it kindles into a greater flame of faith.

In addition, recognizing that each act pleasing to God requires fresh grace, we are reminded not to presume upon our own wisdom, willpower, or strength. We should never boast in our actions but always acknowledge our inherent weakness. In every virtuous deed, we must give all glory to God and maintain ceaseless vigilance in prayer. We are sustained by grace as long as we stand, and to perform one good work after another, we continually depend on the supply of new grace.

Lastly, since God's preceding and active grace transforms our wills, making them from unwilling to most willing, our obedience must be entirely voluntary. Those led by the liberating Spirit of God should willingly and joyfully perform their duties with a ready heart, as if there were no heaven or hell, no judge or judgment awaiting them after this life. They should embrace the Spirit of life within Christ as their guiding law.

The final state is the state of glorification beyond this earthly life. In this state, the freedom of the will consists solely in the inclination to do what is good and pleasing to God. It is the perpetual declaration of the glorified will: "I commit no evil, and I have no desire for it. I do what is good, and I willingly choose it." This is the true freedom in which man's will is harmonized with the free will of God and the righteous angels, all of whom will only that which is good and cannot will anything evil.

With the discussion thus far, it becomes evident that the words from the current text, "and ye would not," pertain to the will of man within the realm of corruption. The voice of the regenerated will declares, "I commit evil, but I do not wish to. I perform good, but not as I truly desire." In contrast, the voice of the corrupted will confesses, "I commit evil, and I intend to do so. I refrain from good, and I choose not to do it." This latter voice is distinctly expressed in the words, "And ye would not."

Now, we turn our attention to the third point—the concord or agreement between both wills. The text states, "I would, ye would not." It is only fair to inquire whether there exists a harmony or agreement between God's will and man's will and how this relates to the text. I reply that there is a profound harmony, and it generally rests in this: God's will holds absolute sovereignty over the will of man, and man's will is entirely subject to it, depending upon it without reservation. Consequently, wherever man possesses a will, God has a prior will, and wherever man's will exerts any influence or action, God's will previously held sway.

Moreover, man's will is dependent on God's will in three significant aspects: sustenance, determination, and regulation or governance. Concerning sustenance, man relies on God's will because his very nature, strength, and every motion hinge upon the divine will. Man's existence could not persist for even a fleeting moment if it were not sustained by God. It might be argued that if God sustains the sinful will, He sustains not only the will itself but also its sin. I counter that God sustains the nature of the will, not the sin within it. Thus, He upholds the will as will, uncontaminated by its corruption or sinfulness. This concept finds its parallel in the realm of nature: when a person limps while walking, the motion of the body emanates from the soul and is preserved by it, but the limping, which accompanies the motion and introduces disorder, does not stem from the soul, nor is it preserved by the soul. Instead, it results from a defect in the leg or foot. This teaches us to recognize God's enduring patience, as He sustains the components of our bodies, our souls, their faculties, and actions, even during our transgressions and affronts to Him.

Secondly, it prompts us to acknowledge the detestable nature of every sin. We sin while under the providence of God, sustained and preserved by Him. In the very actions that we could not perform without His sustaining grace, we commit offenses against Him and kindle His righteous anger.

Additionally, the dependence of man's will on God's will extends to determination. This is because we cannot, and do not, will anything without the will of God. As Christ taught, not even a sparrow lands on the ground "without the heavenly Father" [Matthew 10:29], meaning without His decree or will. The malicious and wicked intentions of the Jews could not even will, let alone carry out, anything against Christ, except for "what the hand and counsel of God had determined to be done" [Acts 4:28]. Furthermore, God determines the will in two distinct ways.

In good matters, God internally motivates and inclines the will towards the willing and doing of the good it desires. Because God's will serves as the primary cause of all good things, man's will relies on it for virtue, application, and the order of operation. In terms of virtue, secondary virtues stem from the primary one. In terms of application, God employs man's will as an instrument of His own will, directing it toward the accomplishment of His intentions, just as a carpenter uses, handles, and applies his tools. In terms of the order of operation, the first cause always initiates the work, and the second does not act without the first. Consequently, the good things that man wills, he wills them in this way because God willed them first. This is why Paul asserts that good works "are prepared by God" [Ephesians 2:10] for us to engage in. Such preparation takes place because God decrees and determines within Himself the accomplishment of all actions.

Conversely, with respect to evil matters, God's determination is to not hinder them as He is able. From this divine will follows sin in the human will as a consequence, not as a direct effect. It is a consequence because when God withholds or withdraws His sustenance and governance from the will, the will can do nothing but lean towards evil, just as a staff in my hand promptly falls when I withdraw my hand. To avoid evil is inherently good; therefore, we cannot avoid the slightest evil unless God enables us to do so. However, evil is not the result of God's will, because God implants nothing in man's will to induce it to will evil. Rather, He simply refrains from providing it with assistance and guidance, which He is not obligated to provide.

Here, we encounter long and intricate debates concerning the harmony between God's divine plan and the freedom of man's will. Some argue that man's will loses its liberty and becomes enslaved when it submits to God's unchanging and necessary decree. In response, I offer the following points. First, when a person's will makes a determined choice, it does not forfeit its liberty. Therefore, it is clear that human will and God's determination can coexist harmoniously. Second, God's decree does not negate liberty; rather, it guides and directs it gently, offering appropriate and suitable objects in accordance with the nature of the will. Consider the necessity of Christ's death according to God's decree—it was necessary. However, when we consider Christ's inherent nature, He could have prolonged His life. Yet, when we examine Christ's will, we see that His death was a free and willing sacrifice. Without this freedom, His death would not have sufficed as atonement for sin. God, too, performs certain actions out of absolute necessity, yet He exercises perfect freedom of will. Therefore, if absolute necessity does not extinguish free will, much less shall conditional necessity, which depends on God's decree, do so. Finally, God's decree actually upholds the liberty of the will. His determination ordains that the operation of secondary causes aligns with their respective conditions: natural causes work naturally, free causes act freely, necessary causes operate necessarily, and contingent causes function variably and contingently. Hence, God's necessary decree ensures that man shall will this or that, not out of necessity on the part of the individual will, but out of freedom.

Thirdly, man's will is subject to the governance of God's will. This divine governance takes two forms. Firstly, God governs the wills of the righteous by working His own good purpose within them and through them. He influences them through His Spirit, causing them to move and incline towards His divine will. Moreover, they serve as holy instruments through which God accomplishes His divine purpose.

Secondly, God exercises His governance over the wills of the wicked and ungodly through six distinct actions.

The first action is permission, where God withdraws His grace from the will. In this state, God does not illuminate the mind nor incline the will but leaves it to its own devices. It's akin to handing the reins over to a wild horse, allowing it to run unchecked.

The second action is the delivery of the will to Satan, a concept found in passages like 1 Corinthians 5:5 and 1 Timothy 1:20. This occurs when God permits the devil to tempt, assail, and trouble the will of man, which has been abandoned to its own sinful devices. This unfortunate state is often experienced by obstinate sinners, and it is something we pray to avoid when we say, "Lead us not into temptation."

The third action involves God ceasing to restrain the corruption of the will, either wholly or partially. It may involve God temporarily withholding restraint as a form of punishment for prior sins, allowing the individual to be ensnared by the lusts of their own heart.

The fourth action is the bending, moving, or inclining of the wicked will. God does not cause sin by inspiring it directly (for that would make Him the author of sin), but rather, He presents objects—whether good or at least morally neutral—in which the will finds opportunities to be obstinate, rebellious, and self-willed. Much like how the heat of one's stomach in winter is intensified by the surrounding cold air, an untrained horse, when spurred due to disobedience, may fling out and unseat its rider. Similarly, the sinful will of man, when confronted with commandments, threats, judgments, promises, and blessings, can become even more sinful and obstinate. This is the situation Paul refers to when he speaks of "sin taking occasion upon the good commandments of God" in Romans 7:8 and 7:13. David also recognized God's role in this dynamic, as seen when he declared that God "moved the hearts" of the Egyptians to hate His people in Psalm 105:25.

The fifth action is ordination, wherein God skillfully employs the wickedness of man's will and directs it towards good purposes, much like a skilled physician might use poison as a remedy. In this sense, Assyria is referred to as the "rod of His indignation" in Isaiah 10:5, and the Medes and Persians are called "His sanctified ones" in Isaiah 13:3. Despite the Jews' collective will to crucify Christ and bring about His death and destruction, God's sovereign will and plan brought about the redemption of mankind through their actions. He accomplishes His divine purposes through the instrumentality of human will, all the while allowing the will to operate freely in its own evil endeavors.

The last action of God involves two scenarios: one in which He graciously turns a person back to Himself from their wickedness out of His boundless mercy, and another in which He opens a way for an individual who, of their own accord, is heading toward wickedness. In the latter case, God allows them to continue down that path, eventually leading to their own destruction as an execution of divine justice. It's akin to a house that is collapsing: rather than providing support or pushing it down, God removes impediments and clears the way, ensuring that when it falls, it does so directly and in alignment with His purposes.

Now, let us turn our attention to the practical applications of the preceding doctrine, which are manifold. Firstly, through this doctrine, we gain a proper understanding of many passages in Scripture. For instance, when the Lord declares concerning Pharaoh, "I will harden his heart" (Exodus 4:21), this is not because God implants hardness in his heart. Instead, God governs Pharaoh's wicked will through various actions, which can be categorized into four aspects.

Firstly, God permits Pharaoh to follow his own sinful inclinations. Secondly, God allows Pharaoh to fall under the influence of the devil and the desires of his own heart. Thirdly, God confronts Pharaoh with a command to release the Israelites, which, paradoxically, only hardens Pharaoh's heart further as he becomes more obstinate and rebellious. Lastly, God utilizes Pharaoh's hardened heart to demonstrate His own justice and judgment, allowing Pharaoh to proceed headlong toward his own destruction.

This perspective also helps us interpret passages where Scripture mentions that "God put a lying spirit into the mouths of the prophets of Ahab" (Ezekiel 14:9) or speaks of God deceiving or giving up individuals to reprobate minds. In such cases, we must understand that God's actions are either permissive or instrumental. He refrains the wicked heart from certain sins while permitting them to indulge in others, or He employs their actions as instruments to achieve His purposes.

Similarly, when Scripture records that "God delivered the wives of David to Absalom" (2 Samuel 12:11) or "stirred up David to number the people" (Genesis 45:5), we should recognize that these events are part of God's providential ordering of human affairs for His divine purposes. Joseph's journey to Egypt also illustrates this concept, as God's providence caused merchants to appear at a crucial moment, leading to Joseph's sale into Egypt, which ultimately served God's greater plan.

Furthermore, some theologians have suggested that God has an applied or depending will, implying that God wants all humans to be saved, but some choose not to be saved, so God chooses some and rejects others based on their willingness. However, in light of the earlier doctrine, this notion appears to be a human invention. In reality, man's will wholly depends on God's will. The Scriptures clearly state that God shapes vessels of honor and dishonor, not by the power of the clay but by the will of the potter. The first cause governs the second, not the other way around. To subordinate God's will to man's will is to diminish God's majestic sovereignty and elevate the creature above the Creator.

Others propose that God's will is dependent on foreknowledge, suggesting that God does not decree specific outcomes for contingent events but rather foresees what creatures will choose in various circumstances and then determines His actions accordingly. However, this viewpoint, while acknowledging a general providence, undermines God's certain determination of all particular events. It is illogical to assume that God foresees the future actions of man's free will when He has yet to determine anything. Events occur because God has already decreed their occurrence, and therefore, God's foreknowledge of future events follows from His divine decree. If God's decree were based on man's prior choices, how could we reconcile this with passages such as "I will cause them to walk in my statutes" (Ezekiel 3:6)? This verse emphasizes that God does not await man's will but subjects man's will to Himself. Even the papists themselves recognize this aspect of God's providence.

Thirdly, considering that man's will is absolutely subject to the pleasure of God, our sacred duty is to willingly submit ourselves to Him in all things whenever His will is made known to us.

Lastly, this doctrine of the alignment and cooperation between man's will and God's will should serve as the foundation of our patience and a source of our comfort. We should recognize that no calamity or affliction befalls us without the divine will being involved. Creatures can neither will nor act against us without it being first ordained by God. Even the devil could not touch Job without divine permission, and he could not enter the herd of swine without God's leave. In this context, we find David saying, "Let Shimei curse, for he curseth because the Lord bid him do so" (2 Samuel 16:10). Similarly, Joseph derives solace for himself and his brethren by acknowledging that it was not they but the Lord who sent him into Egypt.

While there is harmony between God's will and man's will, there is also discord between man's will and God's Word or His revealed will, as evident from the text at hand. Some theologians have introduced the distinction of God's grace into two categories: sufficient and effectual. They argue that sufficient grace allows a person to be saved if they cooperate with it, while effectual grace ensures a person's actual salvation. They maintain that sufficient grace is granted to all at some point, but effectual grace is not.

They support this distinction with examples like the Jews who rejected Christ, asserting that since they were rebuked for their rejection, they must have had sufficient grace. However, this argument does not establish that sufficient grace was given at the time of God's call to the Jews. Furthermore, the objection that God did everything possible to make His vineyard produce good fruit does not necessitate the existence of grace sufficient for salvation that is not effectual. God's actions were sufficient to make a good vineyard bear fruit, but they could not change the nature of a corrupted vine. Similarly, the Lord's waiting for grapes does not imply the granting of sufficient grace at that time.

The argument about Adam receiving sufficient grace but not effectual grace due to his fall is also flawed. Adam had grace sufficient for the perfection of a creature but not for unchangeable perseverance, especially in the face of temptation. His grace was effectual in terms of righteousness and happiness but not for persevering in both. Lastly, the objection that God forsakes no one until they first forsake Him is based on a misunderstanding of divine forsaking. God may forsake someone for trial or for punishment. Forsaking for trial precedes human forsaking, as seen with Adam. Forsaking for punishment follows sin, and in such cases, those forsaken by God have indeed first forsaken Him. In summary, there exists a grace that is sufficient for conviction and for leading a moral life, yet it may not be effectual for salvation. However, the grace that truly leads to salvation is both sufficient and effectual, particularly the gift of regeneration, in which God grants not only the capacity for conversion but also the will and the action itself.

Now, let us explore the fourth point of consideration – how Christ willed the conversion of Jerusalem. His desire for their conversion was driven by love and patience. His love is exemplified in two distinct ways. Firstly, even though He was God, possessing all majesty, and humanity was comprised of wretched sinners, His natural enemies, He willingly embraced a lowly and humble state to be like a hen to the Jews. Secondly, He assumed the qualities, disposition, and tender affection of a mother hen towards her chicks.

To better grasp these concepts, we must address three key questions. Firstly, is there an affectionate love in God akin to that found in humans and animals? Affections of creatures are not directly applicable to God since they bring about changes, and God is unchanging. Thus, all affections and love attributed to God are done so metaphorically, for two reasons. Firstly, God possesses an unchanging nature that takes pleasure in all good things and possesses a will that earnestly desires the preservation of all good things. This nature and will of God make the best love in creatures seem like a mere faint shadow. Secondly, love is attributed to God because He performs actions that love prompts creatures to undertake, as He bestows blessings and benefits upon His creation, just as a lover does for the beloved. All other affections are similarly ascribed to God, but in this figurative sense.

The second question pertains to whether God harbors hatred towards His creatures, considering the comparison to a hen's love for her young. To address this, we must distinguish between human passion and divine providence and justice. Hatred as a passion is not applicable to God, but in terms of providence and justice, it can be understood in three ways. Firstly, in Scripture, hatred can signify a withholding of love and mercy, as when it is stated that those who follow Christ must "hate father and mother," meaning they should prioritize Christ over their familial bonds. In this sense, hatred can be attributed to God, as He is said to love Jacob and hate Esau – not that He utterly despises Esau, but rather that He does not love Esau with the same fervor as Jacob. Secondly, there exists in God a nature that abhors and detests iniquity. As the psalmist proclaims, "God loves righteousness and hates iniquity." God's hatred in this context is not directed towards humanity in general but towards sin and iniquity, which stem from the work of the devil within man. Thirdly, God punishes and disciplines wrongdoers, and it is in this aspect that He is said to hate them. As David states, "God hates the workers of iniquity and destroys those who speak lies." Thus, we discern two degrees of hatred in God – a negative one in which God withholds His special love from some while granting it to others based on His divine pleasure, and a positive one when He hates and detests His creatures. The latter always arises due to sin, while the former precedes sin. In the text at hand, where God is likened to a hen who loves and gathers all her chicks, we must understand that this pertains to Christ's dealing not with all of humanity but specifically with His own church. He calls all outwardly through the proclamation of His word and outwardly incorporates them into the covenant. In light of these insights, we are instructed, following God's example, to abhor and detest iniquity while consistently distinguishing between the individual and the sin committed.

Now, let's explore the third question: In what manner is Christ like a hen to His church? Christ resembles a protective hen to His church in various aspects. He provides temporal blessings and deliverance; He offers comfort during afflictions and numerous corrections. However, His most significant role lies in His word, which He imparts through the ministry of the prophets. This word is like the outstretched wing under which He shelters His people, and it is the voice through which He calls and beckons them to Himself.

Having unraveled the meaning of this similitude, we can now turn our attention to its practical implications. Through this comparison, we gain insight into the tender love of God for His church and land. He has generously presented us with the gospel of salvation for over forty years, extending His arms of mercy to embrace us and covering us with His protective wing. This profound love calls for our hearts to overflow with love for Christ and our mouths to resound with praise.

Moreover, we glean from this analogy that the gospel brings with it all the other blessings of God. By embracing the gospel, we invite God's kingdom, which encompasses all the blessings necessary for our well-being. The peace and protection enjoyed by our church and land, preserving us from becoming prey to our adversaries, stem from the gospel of life. Consequently, the notion held by certain individuals within the papal tradition that the world was more prosperous in the past, under what they refer to as the "old learning" or "old religion," is both foolish and false.

Additionally, we are reminded that if we desire all essential blessings in this life, our primary step should be to embrace the gospel of Christ.

Furthermore, if Christ assumes the role of a hen, we must adopt the disposition of the chicks in relation to Christ. This entails three important aspects. Firstly, we must allow ourselves to be gathered to Christ, turning away from our sins, placing our faith in Him, aligning our minds and dispositions with His, and permitting Him to infuse us with His heavenly and spiritual life, much like a hen cherishing her chicks by brooding over them. Secondly, we must diligently heed Christ's word and obey His will, just as the chicks respond to the call of the hen, allowing Him to govern both our hearts and our lives in every aspect. Lastly, we should depend on Christ's sweet and merciful promises, seeking refuge under His wing against the forces of hell, Satan, death, and damnation.

Indeed, anyone among us who fails to earnestly fulfill these three duties to Christ, despite His merciful and tender love extended to us over these forty years, stands as nothing less than a rebellious ingrate.

Now, let us explore the topic of Christ's patience, as expressed in these words: "How often would I?" The underlying meaning is this: "You have consistently provoked Me with your sins throughout time, yet I have not withdrawn My love from you. Instead, I have repeatedly sent My prophets to call and gather you back to Me." This demonstration of God's patience serves to accentuate Jerusalem's rebellion, and it warrants further discussion.

Firstly, we may inquire whether the virtue of patience found in humans is also present in God. In a strict sense, it is not, as human patience often involves enduring passions and suffering. God, however, is not subject to any passions or suffering, given His unchanging nature. Furthermore, what is truly within God is eternal, while this form of patience is temporal, existing only for the duration of this world. Nevertheless, the Scriptures attribute this patience to God for two reasons.

The first reason is rooted in God's infinite goodness of will and nature, which dictates that He never desires the absolute perdition or destruction of any creature. As stated by the prophet Ezekiel, "God does not delight in the death of a sinner." When Scripture mentions that vengeance belongs to God and He will repay, it should be understood in the context of God seeking to execute justice through the punishment of sin, rather than His intent to destroy. Some may argue that God is depicted as "making vessels of wrath prepared for destruction." In response, I would caution a careful and cautious interpretation of this passage. I believe it signifies that God designates vessels for wrath through His will and decree, indicating His choice to pass over and forsake some individuals in terms of His love and mercy. This divine act of passing over effectively designates them as vessels for wrath. However, God does not unleash His wrath upon them in secret and righteous judgment until they have been tainted by their own iniquity. Thus, although they are prepared for destruction, they are only truly destroyed due to their own sins.

In light of this incomprehensible and excellent goodness of God, which far surpasses the virtue of human patience, God is described as patient. His patience stems from this divine goodness, which serves as the archetype, while human patience is but a feeble reflection.

The second reason why God is described as patient is because He engages in actions akin to what patient individuals do. Firstly, He extends invitations to men for repentance; secondly, He promises forgiveness; thirdly, He delays punishment; fourthly, initially, He inflicts milder penalties, which, if unheeded, escalate to harsher consequences; and finally, when there is no hope of amendment, He enforces eternal death and destruction.

The purpose of God's patience is twofold: first, to gather and call the elect of God; and second, to eliminate all excuses from the ungodly, as emphasized in verses 22–23.

God's patience can be categorized as either universal or particular. Universal patience applies to all men. The decree of divine justice was declared to Adam and, through him, to all of humanity: "When you eat of the forbidden fruit, you shall surely die" [Genesis 2:17], signifying both physical and spiritual death. Dathan and Abiram were swiftly swallowed by the earth as a result of their rebellion [Numbers 16:23]. Fire from heaven consumed the captains and their fifties upon their disobedience to Elias. Thus, every sin merits immediate destruction, and for each transgression committed, we deserve a corresponding condemnation. One might inquire why God does not execute His decree immediately. The answer lies in God's just remembrance of His mercy, where His justice yields to His mercy. God has another decree of mercy that He is determined to fulfill alongside the decree of justice, such as the promise that "the seed of the woman shall bruise the serpent's head" and "Ask of me, and I will make the nations your heritage, and the ends of the earth your possession." To manifest His mercy upon humanity, God's justice is executed with great patience, proceeding through various stages. This patience extends to all people, without exception, who are descendants of Adam through generation.

Special patience, on the other hand, pertains to specific individuals or regions. For instance, God delayed the flood for 120 years, showing patience towards the people of the old world. He deferred judgment on the Amorites until their iniquities reached their full measure. The Egyptians were spared for four hundred years, and Israel's idolatry was tolerated for 390 years before their punishment through seventy years of captivity. God patiently overlooked the ignorance of the Gentiles for four thousand years, and the destruction of Antichrist will not occur until the coming of Christ. When individuals blaspheme God and Christ through oaths invoking wounds, blood, heart, sides, nails, life, according to their deserts, they should quickly descend to hell. Yet God withholds His judgment, granting some of these individuals the grace of true repentance. Even the least offender on Earth partakes in God's great patience, as He sustains the functions of our bodily members, the faculties and movements of the soul, even during actions that offend Him. The extent of this divine longsuffering is beyond human comprehension.

The purpose of God's patience becomes evident. Firstly, it serves as a teacher for all to turn to God through genuine repentance. As Romans 2:4 tells us, "Do you presume on the riches of his kindness and forbearance and patience, not knowing that God's kindness is meant to lead you to repentance?" God is patient with us, desiring none to perish but for all to come to repentance. Presently, this is a time of visitation for us, the English nation, a span of over forty years during which God has persistently called upon us with great patience, knocking at the doors of our hearts and extending His arms of mercy. Therefore, it is the collective duty of the English people to turn to God with all their hearts, adhering to the entirety of God's law. Isaiah's words reflect our present obligation: "Seek the Lord while he may be found; call upon him while he is near" [Isaiah 55:6]. To motivate our lethargic souls, we can consider several reasons. First, the duration of God's patience is unknown to us, and when individuals, abusing His patience, proclaim "peace, peace," sudden destruction awaits, comparable to labor pains in childbirth. Therefore, we must make the most of our time, as Peter advises, "The day of the Lord will come like a thief, and then the heavens will pass away with a roar, and the heavenly bodies will be burned up and dissolved, and the earth and the works that are done on it will be exposed" [2 Peter 3:10]. Second, the longer God's patience prevails, the greater His wrath becomes. A blow, when delayed, intensifies in impact. Indeed, God's wrath is inherently dreadful, surpassing the wrath of a lion, a prince, or any other creature. Compared to God's wrath, even the wrath of all creation is like a drop of water in the vast sea. Mountains melt before His indignation, and the heavens and elements will melt at His coming, much more so will our stony hearts. Third, God has a treasury and storehouses of judgment, into which unceasing sinners deposit wrath and judgments, reserved for the day of reckoning [Romans 2:5]. When individuals wholeheartedly turn from their wicked ways, this treasury is emptied, as seen in the example of the Ninevites. Therefore, all, from the highest to the lowest, should reflect upon their transgressions, recognizing how they have misused God's merciful patience, and hasten to turn to God and Christ, our merciful Savior. Some may claim that they do not abuse God's patience and have repented long ago. In response, it must be acknowledged that the number of those who genuinely turn to God in their hearts is relatively small, like gleanings compared to the entire harvest. Others may argue that they are not like the Jews who deny Jesus Christ as the Messiah. However, while we may confess Christ verbally, many among us deny Him through their actions and sinful lifestyles. Apart from the sins of the second table, five prominent transgressions prevail among us. Firstly, willful ignorance, as many display little or no concern for knowing God and His path of righteousness. Secondly, the irreverent disregard for the gospel, with obedience to its blessed doctrine and even the mere profession of it often labeled as "preciseness." The gospel's profession occasionally serves as a subject of mockery, potentially indicating its departure from our midst. Thirdly, worldliness has assumed control, as if this world were the only one, and heaven were located on earth. Fourthly, lukewarmness prevails, with many remaining indifferent to their own spiritual condition, oblivious to their spiritual destitution, and unaware of their dire need for the blood of Christ. Consequently, they profess their faith formally, not sincerely, merely complying with the good laws of a righteous ruler. Lastly, hypocrisy is widespread, as those who partake in the Lord's Supper, a pinnacle of earthly Christianity, profess their union with Christ and their fellowship with Him. However, most individuals, having distanced themselves from this holy sacrament, live as they please, showing disdain for those who do not conform to their ways. These are but some of the common fruits in our English vineyard [Song of Solomon 4:16]. It is imperative for all of us to beseech God to breathe upon His vineyard so that it may yield better fruit and avert the impending judgments.

Secondly, as we observe God's remarkable patience towards us, we are instructed to cultivate patience in our own lives, especially when we encounter trials and divine corrections. When God places His hand upon us, we should not respond with anger, frustration, or rebellion, but rather maintain a quiet and submissive heart in accordance with His will, even when the hardships are severe and prolonged. In Scripture, this patient submission to God is often described as "the silence of the heart," signifying a heart that, without protest or complaint, yields itself to God's sovereign purposes in all circumstances. We find counsel in Psalm 4:4, which advises us to "ponder in your own hearts on your beds, and be silent," and in Psalm 37:7, which encourages us to "be still before the Lord."

Thirdly, given God's remarkable patience toward humanity, it is only fitting that we extend patience and forbearance to one another. As the apostle Paul exhorts us, "Be kind to one another, tenderhearted, forgiving one another, as God in Christ forgave you" [Ephesians 4:32]. Our faith in God's merciful patience naturally leads to the development of patience and longsuffering in our relationships, particularly in dealing with anger and the desire for vengeance.

Lastly, considering that God calls us to salvation with great patience, we must also exhibit patience in our response to His call and in the pursuit of our own salvation. We must attentively listen to His word and, with patience, produce the fruit of righteousness [Luke 8:15]. Our prayers must be marked by unwavering perseverance, as illustrated by the Canaanite woman who persistently sought Christ's help [Matthew 15:26]. Our hope must be sustained through patience and the comfort derived from the Scriptures [Romans 15:4]. In summary, we cannot attain the promises of God without enduring patience [Hebrews 10:36].

The fifth and final aspect to consider is the meaning of "the children of Jerusalem." In biblical context, the term "children" encompasses four distinct concepts. Firstly, some individuals are children by means of biological descent, as indicated in Luke 3, where an extensive genealogy traces lineage from Adam to Christ. Secondly, certain people are regarded as children through adoption, even in the absence of biological connection. For example, Michal, who never bore children during her lifetime, is credited with bearing five children to Adriel because she adopted and raised his offspring as her own [2 Samuel 6:23; Numbers 21:8]. Thirdly, individuals are referred to as children in the context of legal inheritance, denoting their right to particular possessions or titles. An instance is found in Zedekiah, who, despite being the uncle of Jehoiakim, is termed the son of Jehoiakim because he succeeded Jehoiakim as the next heir to the throne in the kingdom of Judah [2 Kings 24:17; 1 Chronicles 3:16]. Jeconiah (Coniah) was childless [Jeremiah 22:30], yet he is said to have fathered Salathiel because Salathiel was the designated successor to the throne of Judah, being the closest in David's lineage. Finally, individuals are called children in relation to certain attributes, qualities, or affiliations, much like how children belong to their parents. For instance, people may be referred to as children of light, darkness, sin, or wrath. In this text, the inhabitants of Jerusalem are denoted as the children of the city, reflecting their affiliation with and identity as its residents.

With due reflection upon the rebellion of Jerusalem, we now turn our gaze to the impending punishment, which proclaims, "Behold, your habitation shall be left to you desolate," signifying that both the city and the temple will become a barren wasteland.

It is imperative to first acknowledge that the punishment for Jerusalem's rebellion is a predetermined desolation, encompassing both the city and the sacred temple. This contemplation serves as a poignant mirror for our English nation, offering a glimpse into our potential future unless we repent for our ingratitude toward God's blessings and bear forth more fruitful expressions of the gospel than is common among us. Much like the old world that heedlessly disregarded the ministry of

Noah, the proclaimer of righteousness, and consequently faced devastation through a worldwide deluge, it is a universal divine decree that reads, "The nations and kingdoms that refuse to serve you shall perish and be utterly destroyed" [Isaiah 60:12]. If God did not spare the natural branches, how much less leniency shall be shown to us, mere wild branches, if we persist in our neglect and casual disregard for the Gospel of salvation, a sin far too prevalent in our midst.

Secondly, the impending desolation of Jerusalem serves as a mirror to each one among us who, in this era of God's gracious visitation, belittles or dismisses the ministry of the gospel. For those who do not mend their ways and do so promptly, complete desolation will inevitably befall them and their households. God has passed His unambiguous judgment: "Those who distance themselves from God shall perish" [Psalm 73:27]. Indeed, those who distance themselves from God are those who cannot bear to embrace fellowship with Him through His word and submit themselves to its authority.

Thirdly, it becomes evident through this contrast that the stability of all earthly kingdoms is contingent upon obedience to the gospel of Christ. God's kingdom is the epitome of steadfastness, impervious to any threat. When the gospel is heeded and obeyed within a kingdom, it finds its foundation in the dominion of God Himself.

Furthermore, this desolation is both enduring and awe-inspiring. It endures until the final judgment, for it is written that Jerusalem shall be "trodden under foot until the time of the Gentiles be fulfilled" [Luke 21:24], a time that heralds signs in the sun and moon, accompanied by the shaking of the powers of heaven—an event that precedes the last judgment. Consequently, it becomes evident that neither the city of Jerusalem nor its temple exists today. Some might argue that they could have been rebuilt since their destruction, but due to God's curse, such an endeavor is rendered impossible. History attests to this, as three centuries after the death of Christ, the Jews, with the assistance and permission of Emperor Julian, sought to rebuild their temple and city, only to be thwarted by divine intervention, including thunder, lightning, earthquakes, and the loss of many lives. It may also be noted that the city presently referred to as Jerusalem is either a city in ruins or Bethara, a fortified city established by Emperor Hadrian.

Secondly, this revelation underscores the futility of the wars waged in the past to reclaim the Holy Land and Jerusalem. Such endeavors were the result of papal policies, designed to strengthen the Pope's influence in Europe. Yet, there was little promise of good in a place cursed with perpetual desolation. Thirdly, it becomes clear that pilgrimages to the Holy Land are superfluous. Lastly, we can deduce that antichrist will not reign in the temple at Jerusalem—a notion rooted in erroneous beliefs. How can he sit in a temple that lies in utter ruin, where not a stone rests upon another? It is argued that antichrist will destroy the two prophets of God "in the city in which Christ was crucified" [Revelation 11:8; Acts 9:5]. However, Christ is crucified not only in His person but also in His members, and in this regard, He was and continues to be crucified in Rome, where His members have suffered even more extensively than in Jerusalem.

Furthermore, this desolation was profoundly horrifying, and the tribulation it entailed surpassed any in history [Matthew 24:21]. Historical records attest to its magnitude. During the siege of Jerusalem, the city was first besieged by Titus Vespasianus's army, known as "the abomination of desolation." It was encircled by a wall with thirteen fortifications that commanded the entire city. The Jewish population experienced a grievous famine, resorting to eating old shoes, leather, hay, and animal dung. Approximately 1.1 million of the impoverished perished—some by the sword, others from famine. On one night alone, 2,000 people were disemboweled, and 6,000 perished in a temple porch fire. The entire city was ransacked, burned, and leveled to the ground, with 97,000 taken captive to endure ignoble and wretched servitude.

This gruesome desolation serves as a potent reminder for us to revere and fear God, to wholeheartedly submit to Christ, and as the psalmist wisely implores, to "kiss the Son lest He be angry" [Psalm 2:12], lest we perish along the way when His wrath suddenly ignites.

Concerning this desolation, there are three aspects addressed by Christ. Firstly, He declares it, stating, "Your house shall be left to you desolate." This highlights the providence of God regarding events that come to pass, emphasizing that God is indeed in control. The second aspect is that the rise, continuation, and end of kingdoms are determined by God. As seen in examples like Cyrus acknowledging that "the God of heaven has given me all the kingdoms of the world" [Ezra 1:2] and Daniel's words to Nebuchadnezzar, "The God of heaven has given thee kingdom, power, and glory" [Dan. 2:37], it becomes evident that the disposition of kingdoms is in God's hands. The handwriting on the wall before Belshazzar further illustrates this divine involvement, indicating that his kingdom was numbered and weighed for its continuation or downfall, a message directly from God [Dan. 5:26-28]. This should prompt all righteous citizens of England to earnestly seek God's favor for the preservation of peace and protection for their church and land.

Secondly, Christ reveals the desolation of Jerusalem with absolute certainty, even specifying the precise timing, stating, "This generation shall not pass till all these things be fulfilled" [Matt. 24:34]. As history attests, all these predictions were fulfilled within the span of forty years. This underscores the divine origin and truth of the Gospel of Matthew and others like it, for if a document accurately foretells specific events, it can only be deemed the word of God.

Lastly, Christ endeavors to lead the Jews to a profound contemplation of their impending punishment, as indicated by His use of the word "Behold." It's as if He gently takes them by the hand and urges them to confront their imminent suffering directly. This approach has been a consistent method employed by God throughout history, even before

Adam's fall, when He warned, "If thou eat the forbidden fruit, in dying thou shalt die" [Gen. 2:17]. This deep reflection on the consequences of deserved punishment serves a significant purpose. It serves as a catalyst for repentance [Amos 4:12] and, if not repentance, at least a deterrent against open wickedness. Additionally, contemplating eternal punishments helps us endure the lesser hardships of life with patience. Therefore, it is crucial for people today to earnestly discuss and contemplate the reality of hell and its torments, as this awareness can lead to more genuine repentance and righteousness. Unfortunately, this essential reflection is often hindered by the blindness of human understanding and false notions that make people believe they can easily escape the judgments and punishments of God [Isa. 28:18].

Deo Gloria.

Made in the USA
Middletown, DE
04 February 2024

49087074R00051